Premarital and Remarital Counseling

Premarital and Remarital Counseling

The Professional's Handbook

Robert F. Stahmann

William J. Hiebert

Jossey-Bass Publishers • San Francisco

Substantial discounts on bulk quantities of Jossey-Bass books are available to corporations, professional associations, and other organizations. For details and discount information, contact the special sales department at Jossey-Bass Inc., Publishers (415) 433–1740; Fax (800) 605–2665.

For sales outside the United States, please contact your local Simon & Schuster International Office.

Jossey-Bass Web address: http://www.josseybass.com

 Manufactured in the United States of America on Lyons Falls Turin Book. This paper is acid-free and 100 percent totally chlorine-free.

Library of Congress Cataloging-in-Publication Data

Stahmann, Robert F.
    Premarital and remarital counseling : the professional's handbook
    /Robert F. Stahmann, William J. Hiebert.—1st ed.
      p.   cm.
    Includes bibliographical references and index.
    ISBN 0-7879-0845-2 (alk. paper)
    1. Marriage counseling.   2. Marriage.   3. Remarriage.
  I. Hiebert, William J., date.   II. Title.
HQ10.S69   1997
362.82'86—dc21

        96-49300
        CIP

FIRST EDITION
PB Printing 10 9 8 7 6 5 4 3 2

Contents

*To those who desire
to strengthen premarital and marital relationships,
their own or others'.*

Preface

Recently, while walking down the street in a vacation town, one of the authors noticed a pickup truck with a camper on it. Truck campers were common on the street, but what caught his eye was a large sign on the back of this particular camper: "JUST MARRIED!!" The following, smaller hand lettering preceded those words:

> They donned their best duds and hoped for no hail.
> They'll say their "I Do's," then they're hitting the trail.
> It took him some time, though she never varied.
> Having courted a decade they're finally,
> JUST MARRIED!!

As he took a photograph of the sign on the truck, the author noticed the personalized license plate: 2 WLD 4U.

What a find! We were immersed in writing this book and contemplating the diversity and similarity, the unpredictability and predictability of marriages and remarriages, and here it was summarized on the back of the camper! Marriage is a unique yet common experience. The reasons for and the routes to marriage differ for each couple. Yet there are amazing similarities and patterns among couples. Getting married and being married are very private and also very public situations.

Today, nearly half of weddings are not first-time marriages for at least one member in the couple. We hear almost daily about the high divorce rate in the United States. We agree that it is a tragedy. Yet it is estimated that 90 percent of adults will marry and that 75 to 80 percent of those who divorce will remarry. Marriage is popular.

This book attempts to capture the paradoxes of marriage and to enhance premarital and remarital counseling. Our primary goal is to provide a useful guide to the process and content of such counseling. We have written the book for professionals who do this type of counseling, with a sensitivity to the interdisciplinary backgrounds and settings of those who provide this service. We are aware that clergy do most of the premarital and remarital counseling in the United States, but we know that many other counselors are also involved. Therefore, in this book we have attempted to speak across religious settings and professions to address all those wishing to enhance or begin premarital and remarital counseling.

We have divided the book into three parts. We suggest that the reader read the entire book. It starts with background ideas and information (Part One), then presents the core of our approach to premarital and remarital counseling (Part Two), and finally considers specific topics and interventions (Part Three). We hope that the reader will find the book a useful reference on specific topics and methods in working with engaged and remarrying couples. Our intent is not only to introduce specific information and ideas, but also to enhance and stimulate new approaches to premarital and remarital counseling.

February 1997   Robert F. Stahmann
                                                        Provo, Utah
                                                        William J. Hiebert
                                                        Rock Island, Illinois

Part One

Foundations

Chapter One

Developments in Premarital and Remarital Counseling

Today in the United States, for every hundred weddings, fifty-four are first marriages for both partners and forty-six are marriages in which at least one partner has been married previously.[1] This is the most significant development in premarital and remarital counseling—the increasing numbers of remarriages and of couples seeking counseling to enhance upcoming marriages. Of the forty-six remarriages, eleven are first marriages for the brides and remarriages for the grooms. Another eleven are remarriages for the brides and first marriages for the grooms. The remaining twenty-four are remarriages for both the brides and grooms. Keep in mind that although the majority of people remarrying have divorced or have annulled earlier marriages, these statistics also include widows and widowers.

These days the median age at first marriage for women is about twenty-four; for men it is about twenty-six. The median age at remarriage for divorced people is thirty-four for women and thirty-seven for men. In terms of remarriage for widows and widowers, the median age is fifty-four for women and sixty-three for men.

In 1970, 69 percent of weddings were first marriages and 31 percent were remarriages. Of that 31 percent, about seven weddings would have been a first marriage for the bride and a remarriage for the groom. Another seven would have been a remarriage for the bride and a first marriage for the groom. This leaves about seventeen weddings as remarriages for both the bride and groom. In 1970, the median age at first marriage was about twenty-one for women and about twenty-three for men. The median age when previously divorced people married again was thirty for women and thirty-five for men. For those whose spouses had died, the median age at remarriage was fifty-one for women and fifty-nine for men.

While the premarital counselor may find these statistics interesting in and of themselves, more importantly they show that the population seeking premarital and remarital counseling could be quite diverse. The couples who marry today not only have different marital histories but also come from families with varying marital arrangements. Each partner may be from a family where the parents have remained married, or one reconfigured by divorce or death. Therefore the counselor working with premarital and remarital couples must be sensitive to each partner's relationship history and to the couple's individual and joint expectations for their upcoming marriage.

Several recent studies about premarital counselors[2] reflect that between 30 and 40 percent of those seeking premarital counseling have been married before. These counselors report that this is a significant change, that today many more people are seeking remarital counseling than did a few years ago.

In the decade since the earlier edition of this book was published, there have been great strides in the continual development of premarital and remarital counseling. Several significant studies about those preparing for marriage and those providing marriage preparation programs have emerged. Many churches of various denominations make it possible or requisite for those desiring to be wed in the church to participate in a marriage preparation program or in counseling. Major premarital assessment instruments have been developed, revised, and administered to tens of thousands people preparing for marriage. Information from these assessment instruments has helped the premarital couples and has also yielded insights into the process of marriage preparation itself.

Premarital counseling or education is a widely accepted idea. Most married people—young and old—surveyed by us and others say that some form of premarital counseling or education would have been valuable and they would have participated if it had been offered to them. The majority of persons who have participated in marriage preparation programs feel that this participation was valuable, especially early in their marriage.[3] Today many newly married couples have participated in a marriage preparation program or read a book or magazine articles about marriage before their wedding. Marriage and family life (parenting) are hot topics, as evidenced by the numerous recent books on those and related topics in most bookstores and libraries.

Demographers substantiate that the overall marriage and divorce rates have recently leveled off. The divorce rate for 1995 was reportedly the lowest in over two decades.[4] Yet some 1,169,000 divorces were granted in 1995. Thus, while there is good news that the divorce rate is plateauing or slightly decreasing, the almost million and a quarter divorces represent a significant amount of personal pain and loss for those involved.

What follows in this book is an attempt to bring together the current ideas and information about premarital counseling. We first discuss the background and history of premarital counseling. Then we present characteristics of healthy and well-functioning premarital and interpersonal relationships as a foundation for the counseling process that we develop throughout the book.

History of Premarital Counseling

Today, as in the past, there are three main groups that provide most premarital counseling: clergy, mental health workers, and physicians. Clergy perform the greatest amount of formal premarital counseling, as part of an optional or mandatory marriage preparation program before a church wedding. Clergy also perform the majority of first marriages and remarriages. Mental health counselors do some premarital counseling, often for those who have been divorced and are preparing to marry again. Physicians do some premarital counseling as well, but that is usually limited to one meeting where they give contraceptive and sexual information.

The first documented premarital intervention was in 1924 when Ernest Groves taught the first course in preparation for family life at Boston University.[5] The first mention of premarital counseling as a significant process or a valuable service in building emotional and physical health was in a 1928 article in the *American*

Journal of Obstetrics and Gynecology. From that time until the mid-1950s, the primary literature dealing with premarital counseling focused on the physician and the premarital physical examination. In the 1950s, clergy began developing a literature about premarital counseling. Although there is little in the literature about the historical development of premarital counseling, our examination has led us to divide it into two basic segments. The primary shift in emphasis seems to have come after World War II.

Premarital Counseling Before World War II

The professions providing premarital services of one kind or another prior to the war fall into two general categories: counseling professionals and clergy. We want to explore briefly the attitudes of these two professional groups during that period.

Counseling Professionals

From 1900 until the beginning of World War II, psychology as a discipline and profession was coming into its own. With Freud and his contemporaries came the development of theoretical schools in the understanding of the human personality. To establish itself as its own discipline and profession, psychology had to separate itself from medicine. There was a struggle between the two professions over the supremacy and validity of psychology. But psychological thought, at least in its initial stages, was part and parcel of the medical world. Being essentially oriented toward repairing pathology and the dysfunctional, the medical framework influenced psychology and its orientation.

With this pathological orientation, the focus of psychology as it was translated into therapy was essentially individual and intrapsychic. This was a natural and logical progression from the medical framework into which psychology was born. There is evidence in the literature that some early twentieth-century theoreticians and clinicians postulated the importance of the family unit and the value of treating more than just the individual. Nonetheless, an interactional focus—the awareness of and concern about what transpires between people—did not seriously enter the psychological world until the mid–twentieth century.

Given its individual, intrapsychic orientation, premarital counseling as we understand it today was hardly in evidence prior to World War II. The individual premarital counselor who had an intrapsychic orientation and worked in a psychological setting would not have seen the couple together and would not have been essentially concerned about their interpersonal relationship. At that time, any problem in the marital relationship was seen as a by-product of a problem within an individual. Neurotic or psychotic individuals caused problematic marriages. If a marriage had not commenced, there could hardly be a problem; the marriage would need to have commenced in order for the problem to have developed. With that understanding, then, the counselor in an exclusively psychological setting would hardly have conducted the kind of premarital counseling we know today.

Clergy

Early in the development of the Christian Church, clergy became involved with premarital couples in one way or another. Although the early Christians saw marriage as a private, noninstitutionalized arrangement entered into with the consent of parents and without the need for priestly or civil authorization, the Christianization of western Europe and the church's entrance into the very fabric of political life changed the involvement of both the state and the church in marriage. Initially the wedding ceremony was without benefit of clergy, but by 398 A.D. the Synod of Carthage assumed the use of a priestly benediction in the ceremony.

As the church and subsequently the state became more involved in marriage, couples began to need their parents' permission to wed. Historically, marriages were arranged. Parents' power to control the lives of unmarried children was unsurpassed. Since children in essence did not have any legal standing or power under the common law of the day, parental control was absolute. Permission also became an issue in regard to the clergy. Several of the early church fathers, such as Ignatius and Polycarp, began urging that couples seek permission to marry not only from parents but also from the bishop.

Civil authorities were also concerned with permitting couples to wed. Not only were the familial and clerical structures hierarchical and monarchical, but the civil structure was as well. As Europe became increasingly feudal, overlords began to demand the right to oppose or consent to a marriage. By the Middle Ages, the concept of requiring a couple to have permission to marry from parents, clergy, and overlords was clearly established.

Another issue was the institutionalization of marriage. Although the early church was frequently negative about marriage, seeing celibacy as the ideal, it became increasingly concerned about the nature of marriage and its relation to and connection with Christian life in general. As theological thought became more concentrated and structured on the issue of marriage itself, the church involved itself more and more with both the wedding ceremony and the nature of the couple's relationship. By 1164, the church had officially established marriage as a sacrament. With this movement came the clergy's special involvement with premarital couples.

This development paralleled the clergy's increased participation with other initiatory sacraments. An example is baptism, a rite of initiation into the life of the church. In the early Christian Church, clergy began educating people about the nature of the rite and its meaning in Christian life. Communion was another kind of initiation, a welcoming into the new status of adulthood in Christian life and church life. A similar educational process about Holy Communion and First Communion developed. Clergy soon began teaching people the meaning of the sacrament before they received it. With these educational patterns established with regard to initiatory rites, it was natural that the clergy should follow a similar process with marriage. In a theological sense, marriage could be viewed as a kind of initiation rite. It brought a man and a woman into a new and different relationship with each other and with God. Thus, clergy began seeing couples prior to the wedding. The prewedding sessions conducted by clergy prior to World War II followed the kind of instructional pattern that was typical of the other initiatory rites. The emphasis was on the nature and meaning of the rite itself: the Christian nature of marriage, the place of religion in the home, and the rehearsal of the wedding rite.

With this brief historical overview, it can be seen that although clergy were involved in prewedding sessions with couples long before secular counseling professionals were on the scene, the nature

of these sessions was considerably different from what we conceptualize today.

Premarital Counseling After World War II

Following World War II, several developments in the field of psychology made an impact both on theories of personality and
human interaction (psychology) and on theories and models of
ministry (theology).

Counseling Professionals

In the 1940s and the 1950s, a new concern developed in the field
of psychology in general, and in clinical practice in particular. As
we indicated earlier, prior to World War II the focus was on individual and intrapsychic problems. With the 1940s and 1950s came
an interest in the behavioral problems of children, which brought
with it a focus on the parent-child relationship. This change had
as its by-product the child guidance movement in America and the
establishment of child guidance centers throughout the United
States. The expanding field of vision, which meant moving away
from the individual and considering the parent-child relationship,
brought a new era of concern about what transpired between people as well as what went on inside people.

With the 1950s and 1960s came another new focus—on schiz-
ophrenia. It was the unsolved problem of psychology and there
were no clear answers about its nature and treatment. Early in this
century, the schizophrenic was examined and understood in indi-
vidualistic, pathological terms. By the 1940s, researchers had begun
to focus on the relationship between the schizophrenic patient and
his or her mother. In the 1950s, researchers studied the relationship between the schizophrenic and his or her father. As a result
of all this work, psychologists had a whole new understanding, not
only of the importance of the interactions among all family members but also of the importance of the interactions between husband and wife. The result of this research became the movement
that is known today as marital and family therapy.

Although much has been done since World War II to expand
the purview of psychology, it should be remembered that these

developments have run parallel to an ongoing interest in the individual and intrapsychic problems. While exciting research has taken place in the field of human interaction, the primary emphasis has remained on the individual and intrapsychic makeup. In spite of the developments in the field of psychology in the 1950s and 1960s, psychology has maintained a pathological orientation. The medical model has been dominant in many schools of thought regarding theories of personality and human interaction. A repair orientation rather than a preventive orientation still dominates the field of psychology, both in general and in the practice of counseling.

As a way of summarizing the historical movement after World War II, we can say that while psychology and psychotherapy still maintained a heavy individual and intrapsychic approach, the development of marital and family therapy focused psychology more on interactional aspects. More important, however, the theory began to shift. As research in marital and family therapy increased, it became evident that marital relationships and their health or lack of health were related to something beyond the mental health of the married individuals. It became clear that it really was possible to have an unhealthy marital relationship between two relatively healthy people.

Even more significant, with the theoretical framework now looking specifically at the interaction within the family and especially within the marital dyad, the relationship itself became an issue of focus. Furthermore, the emphasis was not only on the relationship itself but also on the growing understanding that the marital relationship was not accidental but purposeful. There began to be an acknowledgment that some kind of bond maintained the relationship. Thus, marital and family therapists began to look at the relationship as having existed prior to the wedding. All of this of course set the stage for the increased interest of later marital and family therapists in premarital counseling.

Nonetheless, premarital counseling conducted by professionals was still relatively uncommon in the 1960s. Because interactional theory was still in its infancy in the 1950s and 1960s, clinicians in the field still tended to conceptualize marital problems as the problem of one individual in the relationship. Premarital counseling as we understand it today, therefore, was not a

regular part of professional clinical practice. In 1966, a survey of
the professional members of the American Association of Marriage
and Family Counselors indicated that practitioners of that association performed very little formal premarital counseling.[6]

Clergy

With the developments in the general field of psychology in the
1940s and 1950s came a number of intrusions in the field of theology. Several pioneering members of the clergy had become interested in psychology as a way of expanding and understanding
the nature of ministry. These individuals, with their interest in psychology and theology, initiated a movement that is generally recognized by the name of pastoral counseling.

The pioneering clergy who had much to do with initiating
the pastoral counseling movement were indebted, theoretically
speaking, to psychoanalytic thought. As we indicated earlier,
psychoanalytic thought originated in the medical model and in a
pathological framework. Pastoral counseling therefore developed
a heavy bias toward the pathological orientation and the medical
model. This can be clearly seen in an address given by Robert Laidlow, a psychiatrist in the field of marital therapy. Speaking at a professional meeting in 1948 and discussing the role of clergy in
premarital counseling, Laidlow indicated that their task was to
serve as screening agents and to assess the health of the couples
who planned to marry.[7]

We postulate that with the development of the pastoral counseling movement came the clergy's shift in attitude toward ministry
in general, but specifically toward situations that had a counseling context or quality. The shift was away from the educational,
informational stance outlined earlier and toward a search for
pathology.

The role of the minister as a screening agent became more
pronounced in the literature of pastoral counseling and specifically of premarital counseling in the 1950s and 1960s. In 1953, Paul
Johnson, a pastoral counseling pioneer, indicated that he saw the
pastor as being responsible for a marriage's continuing growth.
Charles Stewart, another early author on counseling in the parish
setting, saw the role of the pastor as that of examining a couple's
maturity and emotional readiness for marriage. Aaron Rutledge,

director of the first marriage counseling program at Merrill Palmer Institute in Detroit, Michigan, also saw the role of clergy and of secular counselors as that of examining a couple's emotional readiness for marriage.

The shift in seminary education and the new emphasis on pastoral counseling in general brought an entirely new dimension to the clergy's role. Now the task was not simply to rehearse the wedding and instruct the couple about the Christian nature of marriage, but also to assess the couple's preparedness for marriage. This accompanied a parallel development—an increasing divorce rate. The belief that a couple who had been thoroughly examined would not be susceptible to divorce gave the clergy the ultimate responsibility for determining the outcome of the marriage.

This development, we suspect, has had a great deal to do with ministers' often demonstrated ambivalence and disillusionment about their role in premarital counseling. On the one hand, pastors are asked to accept people as they are and minister to them at that level; on the other hand, pastors are asked to examine the couple's psychological state and intervene in a relationship that has a certain lack of health. In addition, as representatives both of the church and of the state, ministers are asked to perform the wedding on purely civil grounds. With that three-part mix, the minister who takes seriously all three roles at the same time is likely to have succumbed, in years of ministry, to a state of numbness or helplessness in resolving the dilemma.

Educational and Counseling Emphases

In recent years, there are increasing numbers of academic courses in marriage and family preparation. They are usually at the college level but often exist now at the secondary level as well. As mentioned earlier, the first such course was titled "Preparation for Marriage and Family Living" and was offered at Boston University in 1924 by Ernest R. Groves. In 1929, a similar course was offered at Teachers College, Columbia University. Today, similar courses exist on almost every college and university campus.

Earlier writers saw premarital counseling as primarily an educational and informational service. Butterfield[8] pointed out that just as persons develop skills in social life, so they must develop skills in family life and in functioning well in the marital relationship. He indicated that many young people were disappointed or developed problems in marriage because they brought to it very little in the way of useful skills or helpful attitudes.

Albert Ellis[9] argued that another cause of marital failure was ignorance about the nature of marriage itself. He observed that many people entering marriage do not have even the most elementary preparation for the demands that marriage makes on them. Ellis indicated that it is assumed that newlyweds will automatically know how to adapt themselves to it, when in fact this is often not the case.

Later, following a similar line of thought, Rutledge postulated that although marriage itself could be a maturing process, people must have obtained a reasonable amount of adult growth in order to carry their share of the various responsibilities of marriage. Rutledge identified three basic factors in preparing for marriage: discovery of selfhood, continued growth as an individual, and possession of communication and problem-solving skills. He spoke of the premarital counseling process as opening up these three areas of life for the young couple and projecting the couple into the future, enabling them to foresee the kinds of problems and the many challenges that awaited them in marriage. Rutledge argued that if all clinicians devoted one-fourth of their time to premarital counseling, they could make a greater impact on the health of the country than through all of their remaining therapeutic activities. David Mace[10] challenged marriage counselors to move out of the remedial routine and focus their energies on marriage preparation and marriage enrichment.

We agree in substance with these arguments and strongly support the growing emphasis on preventive premarital education and related educational and enrichment programs. However, it is unlikely that the typical marriage and family therapist will be able to move out of traditional therapeutic or remedial services, because of the great demands for treating marital and family related mental health dysfunctions. Also, it is our observation that many marriage and family therapists and related mental health professionals have difficulty making the transition from an exclusively therapeutic framework to a premarital and remarital counseling framework that combines educational and therapeutic emphases.

The Healthy Premarital and Remarital Couple

Premarital and remarital counseling is typically done with relatively functional and psychologically healthy persons and is designed primarily to enhance and enrich growing relationships and secondarily to treat pathological ones. In remarital counseling, where one or both partners have been previously married, there is the added dimension of dealing with how that experience affects the current premarital relationship. Yet overall the goals of remarital counseling are similar to first marriage premarital counseling, that is, to enhance the couple's premarital relationship so as to continue its development into a satisfactory and stable marital relationship.

In this regard, Robert Lewis and Gaham Spanier, family researchers writing in 1979, identified premarital predictors of two important marital dimensions: quality and stability.[11] Marital quality is the subjective evaluation of the marital relationship (for example, satisfaction and happiness). Marital stability is whether the marriage is intact legally (for example, the couple has not separated or divorced). Looking at dozens of studies, Lewis and Spanier identified four categories of premarital variables as influencing the later quality and stability of marriage.

The first, premarital homogamy, states that the greater the premarital homogamy, or similarity in social and demographic factors, the higher the marital quality. Similarities in the following areas emerge as predictors of marital stability or success: racial background, socioeconomic background, religious denominational affiliation, intelligence level, age, and social status.

The second category relates to similarity of personal and emotional premarital resources and life experiences. Specifically, those resources include a high level of interpersonal skill functioning, good emotional health, a positive self-concept, high educational level, an older age at first marriage, a high social class, a high degree of acquaintance between the partners before marriage, and good physical health.

A third proposition relates to positive parental models. Marital quality and stability were correlated with high marital quality in the family of origin, a high level of happiness in childhood, and positive relationships between the person and his or her parents.

✳ The fourth premarital variable category involves support from significant others. Predictive variables were parental approval of the future mate, the person's liking for the future in-laws, and the support of significant friends for the proposed marriage.

In addition to these four categories, Lewis and Spanier identified four other variables as influencing marital quality and stability. First, the greater the level of conventionality is, the higher the marital quality will be. Second, those whose premarital sexual behavior is consistent with their value system will have higher marital quality than those whose premarital sexual behavior conflicts with their values. The third proposition indicates that couples experiencing premarital pregnancy will have lower marital quality than couples who do not experience it. The final proposition is the most general, yet it sheds light on the premarital relationship—the more the motivation to marry is independent of problematic circumstantial factors, including internal or external pressures, the higher the marital quality will be.

We have summarized the preceding findings because we believe that they can give the counselor a framework in designing the premarital and remarital counseling process. Because this work has been systematically derived from the vast family and sociological research literature, the premarital counselor can appropriately use it in a counseling setting. In later chapters, we will extensively address the very important aspects of mate selection and dysfunctional factors in premarital relationships, and thus do not discuss them here.

Recent research has validated, clarified, and expanded Lewis and Spanier's findings about marital quality and stability. In a 1994 review of fifty years of research, Jeffry Larson and Thomas Holman conclude that there are three major premarital predictors of later marital quality and stability: (1) the couple's background and contextual factors (for example, family of origin, sociocultural factors, and current contexts); (2) individual traits and behaviors that can influence the couple's relationship (for example, emotional health, self-esteem, physical health, and interpersonal skills); and (3) the couple's interactional processes (for example, homogamy, interpersonal similarity of values, attitudes and beliefs, premarital sex and childbirth, and communication skills).[12] Thus, premarital and remarital counseling and related educational programs can help couples identify specific factors about themselves or their relationship that relate to later marital quality and stability and, if needed, help them strengthen or change specific traits, behaviors, or ways of interacting.

Table 1.1 summarizes the Larson and Holman review of premarital factors. This table provides useful information for the practice of both premarital and remarital counseling. Counselors should be aware of the authors' caution in regard to using the table:

> We find it somewhat risky to make suggestions for FLE (family life education) and PC (premarital counseling) when the amount of research on some premarital factors is either limited or somewhat inconsistent. Nevertheless, we feel obligated to cautiously summarize the evidence we have to date on premarital factors affecting marital quality and stability so that this information may be used by FLEs and PCs in teaching and counseling couples preparing for marriage. . . . We have included only factors that have been consistently supported in the research literature. Where there are inconsistent or contradictory findings, we report the findings that we believe are most representative of the literature as a whole.[13]

Just as counselors can benefit from reading and applying results from research studies such as those cited earlier, so can counselors benefit from applying the results of studies and clinical reports found in the many excellent lay and professional books out today. As counselors do such reading, we should ask ourselves, "Is what this author says well founded? What ideas can I glean that could be useful in the premarital and remarital counseling that I am doing?" As we pose such questions, we will find that authors in different settings using varying terms and language often identify premarital and marital factors related to marriage stability and satisfaction that are similar and have corresponding implications for marriage.

Some Assumptions About Counseling and the Counselor

Research studies and clinical feedback have influenced the continuing development of the approaches to premarital and remarital counseling that are presented in this book. The following assumptions underlie these approaches:

- Those who benefit most from premarital counseling must voluntarily seek it rather than be forced into it.
- Premarital and remarital counseling is a developmental process and is designed to assist the couple in enhancing their relationship, rather than being a screening process.
- Premarital counseling is most beneficial if obtained early in the relationship and several months before the wedding.
- Persons requesting premarital counseling should expect to learn about themselves to some extent, but primarily about their relationship and each other.
- Couples and counselors favor conjoint sessions over individual sessions.
- In settings where a team offers premarital counseling, such as is often true in the Catholic Church, a team of clergy, lay couples, and parish staff has been rated as most helpful.
- Assessment instruments contribute to the premarital and remarital counseling process.
- It is important that counselors know information such as that cited earlier in this chapter on topics like marriage quality and stability, as well as content areas suggested in later chapters, and that they use that information in designing and delivering their counseling and education.
- While the number of counseling sessions depends on many factors, there must be adequate time spent in counseling, and it must be spread across an adequate time span so that the partners can experience the process and integrate the information into their lives.
- Postwedding follow-up sessions are an important part of both premarital and remarital counseling.

A word about training to practice premarital and remarital counseling. We are of the opinion that for a person to provide adequately the counseling process described in this book, graduate study at the master's level is necessary. This master's-level training should include at least some graduate training in relationship counseling, marital interaction, family studies, and assessment.

Table 1.1. A Summary of Premarital Factors Predicting Marital Quality and Stability and Implications for Practice.

Category of factor	Subcategory	Factor	Implications for practice
Background and contextual factors[a]	Family of origin	Parental divorce	Assess individual's reaction to divorce; examine attitudes toward commitment and divorce; expose to positive models of marriage.
		Parental mental illness	Assess effect on child and recommend personal or family therapy if necessary.
		Family dysfunction	Assess effect on child and recommend personal or family therapy if necessary.
		Support from parents and in-laws	Encourage seeking parental and in-law support or an understanding of their concerns.
	Sociocultural factors	Age at marriage	Discourage teenage marriage.
		Education[a]	Discuss ramifications of limited education on marriage.
		Income and occupation[a]	Discuss ramifications of limited income on marriage.
		Social class[a]	Discuss ramifications of limited education and income on marriage.
		Race[a]	Discuss ramifications of cultural and subcultural norms about marriage; encourage premarital counseling as necessary.
	Current contexts	Support from friends	Encourage seeking friends' support or an understanding of their concerns.
		Internal and external pressures	Teach stress management, effective coping, and mature decision-making skills.
Individual traits and behavior		Emotional health, self-esteem, neurotic behavior, and depression	Do initial assessment and refer for personal therapy.[b]

Category of factor	Subcategory	Factor	Implications for practice
		Interpersonal skills	Assess skills, especially sociability; teach skills or refer for personal or group therapy or skills training programs.
		Conventionality	Assess conventionality and discuss ramifications of unconventionality on marriage.
		Physical health	Assess health; enhance or remedy as necessary by referral to health professionals.
Couple interactional processes	Homogamy	Similarity of race, socioeconomic status, religion, intelligence, age	Assess similarities and discuss ramifications of dissimilarities on marriage.
	Interpersonal similarity	Similarity of values, attitudes, beliefs, and sex role orientations	Assess similarities and discuss ramifications of dissimilarities on marriage.
	Interactional processes	Acquaintance	Assess depth of acquaintance and encourage seeking deeper acquaintance as necessary.
		Cohabitation	Discuss ramifications of cohabitation as a trial marriage or discourage such cohabitation.
		Premarital sex	Discuss ramifications of premarital intercourse or discourage premarital sexual intercourse.
		Premarital pregnancy and childbirth	Encourage avoiding pregnancy or if pregnant and want to marry, encourage marrying *before* birth of child.
		Communications skills	Assess and teach communication, conflict management, and consensus-building skills.

Note: Because gender differences on each factor have been recognized only recently and results are inconclusive, specific recommendations for males and females have not been made.

[a]Relatively weak predictors.

[b]This refers to a preliminary, screening type of assessment based on a knowledge of abnormal psychology. Only licensed mental health professionals should diagnose psychological disorders.

Source: From "Premarital Predictors of Marital Quality and Stability," by J. H. Larson and T. B. Holman, 1994, *Family Relations, 43,* p. 228. Copyrighted 1994 by the National Council on Family Relations, 3989 Central Ave. NE, Suite 550, Minneapolis, MN 55421. Reprinted by permission.

Clergy and mental health counselors offering premarital and re-marital counseling without such a background have an obligation to receive specialized training before they offer or supervise counseling. Premarital counseling teams, which include lay mentors or others, must include trained clergy or mental health counselors. We do not support the idea of having paraprofessionals or laypeople do premarital counseling unless they are under the close supervision of clergy or professionals trained at the master's level.

In this chapter we have examined the historical development of premarital and remarital counseling in both church and secular settings. We have shown how research on marital quality and stability can be used in the design of the counseling process, and we have offered assumptions that underlie effective premarital and remarital counseling. The next chapter examines some of the forces that bring people to marry and explores various dimensions of marriage.

Chapter Two

Why Marry in the First Place and Why Marry Again

We live in a world of rapidly expanding mechanization. The process of living enmeshes us in a complex network of dependency on electronic devices. Perhaps it is no wonder, then, that we tend to develop a mechanical attitude not only toward the world itself but also toward the delivery of human services. No doubt this accounts for the fact that books, seminars, and conferences in the broad field of counseling concentrate extensively, if not exclusively, on techniques and strategies for change.

We believe that a counselor's theoretical framework directly influences his or her practice. To put it more straightforwardly, what people believe determines what they see, and what they see determines what they do. For that reason, we devote this chapter to developing a theoretical framework for understanding the motivations for marriage, and a conceptual framework for understanding the dynamics of marriage.

If we are going to define, understand, and explain counseling, then we need to articulate an understanding of the nature of marriage. If we are going to have some understanding and awareness of the dynamics of marriage, then we need to have some understanding of premarriage, or the premarital state. Thus, this chapter will focus on (1) the forces that bring a man and a woman toward marriage, and (2) the dynamics and dimensions that develop within marriage.

Illusions About Marriage

People enter marriage with some preconceived notions about it. Men and women moving toward a wedding have many ideas about what marriage is supposed to be like. They dream about marriage, about the way their spouse will behave, about the satisfactions they will experience. In part, these dreams and expectations are propagated by the society in which we live. Many of these dreams are myths, yet countless couples move toward and into marriage believing these false ideas. Since the premarital and remarital counselor is part of the culture in which he or she lives, the counselor's ability to discriminate between the myths and the reality will have a potent effect on his or her attitude toward premarital counseling and its effectiveness. Thus, we turn to an exploration of some illusions about marriage.

"Mate Selection and Marriage Are Accidental"

There is a popular idea that marriage and mate selection are a matter of chance. If the marriage does not work and one or both spouses are unhappy, the fault must lie with chance. It certainly could not be the responsibility of the participants! When listening to people elaborate their belief that marriage is accidental, the authors are reminded of the Midwestern college where, in the early part of this century, administrators would line the boys up in the boys' dorm by height, the girls in the girls' dorm by height, and then send them out of the dormitories in two long columns approaching each other. The person who was walking next to you when the lines joined became your date for the spring banquet. We suspect that many people fantasize about marriage in this manner. From this point of view, certainly, there cannot be any logic in the choices made, or better yet, any responsibility for them.

We believe that the idea of accidental mate selection is nonsense. Mate selection is one of the most accurate choosing processes in which human beings engage. A person chooses exactly the mate they need at a certain point in time. This does not mean that another person in the world could not fulfill some of the same needs as the person selected. It does mean that the partner chosen through the mate selection process reflects the person's needs at that moment. Voltaire said it best: "Every person gets exactly what they want. The trouble is, we did not know what we wanted until we got it." People usually know what they want, at least on some subconscious level. Many, however, prefer to believe that mate selection is accidental. The myth relieves them of responsibility for failing or for taking action.

"Marriage Is Dichotomous"

Another popular idea that society propagates is that marriage is a one-sided or lopsided relationship. This myth says that marriage is uneven and unfair. In the last analysis, says the myth, one person will win and the other will lose.

The belief that marriage is dichotomous is most clearly visible when people discuss a couple who is having marital problems or is divorcing. The discussion will often focus on the one-sidedness or unevenness of the marriage, portraying one partner as bad and the other as good, one as right and the other as wrong, one as intelligent and the other as stupid, one as strong and the other as weak, one as healthy and the other as sick.

Although many marriages appear on the surface to be one-sided, we feel that the couple is usually evenly balanced underneath. For example, on the surface a husband may appear to have a temper, whereas the wife appears to be quiet, nonassertive, and lacking anger. The trained eye, however, will see that she, too, becomes angry and puts the knife in, but in a sneaky way. Thus, while couples often appear to be one-sided, with one person losing, they are usually balanced. Either both win or both lose.

The myth that marriage is dichotomous is society's attempt to inculcate the idea that marriage is nonsense. The biggest temptation, when thinking about marriages, is to believe that what happens between a husband and wife does not make sense, and that if indeed a marriage works, no one knows how or why.

Myths and Counseling

We have addressed these two myths because we think that on a very basic level a counselor's views on marriage and how couples come together will affect his or her attitude toward counseling, how it is done, and in fact, whether or not to do it at all. If a counselor believes that marriage is accidental, premarital and remarital counseling will seem a waste of time. Why spend energy trying to make sense out of something that does not basically and inherently make sense? If marriage is a cruel game of the world, if there is no point to it or plan as to how it works, if it is a matter of luck, then the counselor will be cynical toward the premarital and remarital counseling process and toward marriage itself. Perhaps then the counselor, like the King of Hearts in *Alice in Wonderland,* could lament: "If there is no meaning in it, that saves a world of trouble, you know, as we needn't try to find any."

No doubt, whether a counselor buys into these two myths will depend on personal beliefs about his or her own marital status and family of origin. If a person has been able to make sense out of these personal situations and can see how people fit together and what they do for each other, his or her professional goal will be to find sense, or to make sense, of couples' relationships. If his or her family of origin and marriage do not seem to make sense, and if that person cannot figure out what attracted people to each other in his or her own networks, then counseling others will be difficult because he or she will be cynical or disbelieving.

By this point in the chapter, we hope that we have made our assumptions clear: marriage does indeed make sense and people marry for some purpose. We believe people marry to "get." We also believe people marry to "give." However, we want to underscore that individuals marry in order to do something to, or for, themselves: to grow, to leave home, to have an umbrella to shelter themselves from the world's rains, to take a piggyback ride toward a better future.

Motivating Forces for Marriage

Our assumption that marriage is neither accidental nor dichotomous has been influenced by our clinical practice with the hundreds of couples we have seen in marital, premarital, and remarital counseling. In thinking about these couples and the manner in which they chose each other, we have discovered that the couples were apparently performing a task and were involved in a process. It has struck us that many individuals were trying to initiate growth in some way. Perhaps the growth involved becoming more outgoing, more self-confident, or more intimate, or expanding some other dimension of their personality. They felt that the mate they chose from the millions of individuals available was exactly the person who could provide them with the kind of growth they needed. Some women, for example, seek a particular man who can teach them to be tough, just as some men seek a woman who can teach them to be soft. It almost seems to us that couples in some way choose each other on the basis of their potential to induce change. We agree with others who have said that perhaps marriage is an amateur attempt at psychotherapy.[1]

All of this is a way of saying that we believe marriage is purposeful and feel that an individual chooses another on the basis of the partner's ability to initiate or continue the individual's personal growth. We think couples are involved in a task of healing. It is as if many individuals view themselves as incomplete in some way. Their search for a mate is not haphazard, but is rather based on a deeply intuitive homing device that relentlessly and purposely pursues exactly the kind of person who will stimulate the growth they are seeking.

It is amazing how powerful that homing device can be. People can spot each other across a crowded room at a party or sense something in a person who is only barely visible across a street, and be instinctually drawn to the person and find a way to make the contact. The desire to grow, the desire to be completed in some way, is a powerful force at work in individuals. This force brings people together, binding them in a relationship. The attraction, which often is so powerful during the later stages of the dating process that it can be felt by those outside the relationship, owes some of its strength and energy to the potential for growth and the healing force that are present in the coupling process.

Although we believe that marriage makes sense and that the movement toward marriage is in some way a bid for health, we are aware that the forces that impel people toward each other vary. Some of the psychological forces at work are healthy, and others are not. Some of the forces that drive people toward marriage can precipitate further growth and health, whereas other forces can bring disruption or disappointment. We want now to take a look at some of those forces and comment on them briefly.

Emotional Immaturity

Some families have difficulty completing the task of raising their children. They finish the task physically and see to it that the children have the proper food and shelter to enable them to become adults. But raising children is more than ensuring their physical growth. Raising children to be functioning, healthy adults requires that parents pay attention to the emotional well-being of their children. Families are required both to care for their children and at the same time to urge them to become independent. Families need to give the child enough care and attention so that the child feels wanted and loved. At the same time, parents need to help the child become more self-sufficient, more ready to function on his or her own.

Some families enable their children to go away, to become independent, responsible, functioning adults. Other families hang on, making decisions for their children, interrupting the children's decision-making processes, and continuing to take responsibility for them. These families cripple the children's ability to become independent and responsible. Thus, children enter late adolescence or young adulthood physically ready and able to enter marriage, but still not adult in terms of their own responsibility and decision-making ability. These families have made so many decisions for their children that even as young adults, these sons and daughters still need somebody to help them get up in the morning, to see to it that they go to work, and so on. It is as if these families somehow do not successfully resolve the young people's dependency needs.

These individuals, still wanting to be cared for, still needing their parents to take responsibility, will enter a marital relationship seeking to fulfill those unresolved dependency needs. It is as if they look to the mate to be the good, loving, patient, understanding parent that they did not have or continue to need. The marriage becomes a kind of advanced day-care center where the young adult can continue the growing process. This is a powerful force, impelling toward marriage, or remarriage, people who seek a sense of healing from their family of origin or a previous marriage. They may operate with some illusions about what marriage can do for them.

"I Will Be Different After This Marriage"

There are people whose past experiences have made their relationships with other people painful. They have been bruised in some way, whether in their relationships with their parents, in relationships with their peers, or in a previous marriage. In any case, they enter young adulthood feeling burned, lonely, and unwanted. This lack of satisfaction in relationships can cause them to fantasize about a relationship that might be fulfilling, that might in some way heal the pain of their previous relationships.

Marriage or remarriage looms on the horizon as the great possibility, the solution to the hurts of previously painful relationships. People frequently expect that the mate will change them and that marriage will in some way supply the caring and loving environment that will resolve their loneliness and hurt. During the dating process, they do not perceive that marriage might exaggerate the loneliness or make it even worse through the years. Thus, the drive to find a mate who will make one well, whole, and no longer lonely is a powerful force propelling people toward marriage. The same dynamic can make a person divorce one partner and seek another, "different" marriage that they fantasize will be "better."

"Everybody Ought to Be Married"

Because human beings live not in isolation but in society, they experience pressure from society to model their behavior on others' actions. The United States has a marrying culture. Although divorce statistics are high, so are marriage statistics. Approximately nine out of every ten adults will marry. Our society expects people to marry and in some subtle ways discriminates against those who do not.

Some people move into marriage to meet that societal expectation. They want to fit in, sense that they belong, and feel "normal." Self-esteem is important for individuals. Most persons do things that will enhance the way others see them. Because of our societal expectation of marriage, some individuals marry not so much because they wish to be with the person they have chosen, but because they want society's esteem. They seek the approval of parents, friends, and peers who think favorably about marriage and who are usually married themselves. To feel that they are worthy, some individuals move toward marriage.

"Marriage Makes Me an Adult"

We have already discussed families who have difficulty letting their children go. These families hang onto their adult children. In families like these, marriage often becomes a rite of passage. In other words, marriage becomes an act that sons and daughters engage in to separate from their family of origin.

In a way, marriage is one of life's "rule changers." As the birth of a child into the family changes the "rules" about how mother and father relate to each other, so marriage also changes the "rules" concerning how a child relates to parents. When young adults have difficulty taking charge of their own lives, when parents still try to run their adult children's lives, the young individuals may marry in an attempt to change the family's rules. Marriage thus becomes a bid for adulthood.

Counselors often observe that the more enmeshed or overly close the family of origin is (the more reluctant it is to let its children go), the higher the probability is that the adult child will choose a prospective mate who the parents will find undesirable in some way. The more undesirable the mate appears to them, the more the adult child hopes he or she will break the parents' hold. Thus, the bid for adulthood can be a powerful force impelling people toward marriage if they are attempting to separate themselves from controlling parents.

Sexual Urges

Most of us are born into families. In that context, we are cared for in infancy in ways that are both physically and emotionally close. As infants, we receive both physical attention and emotional attention (affection). As a child moves from infancy to childhood to adolescence, that physical and emotional closeness begins to change. About the time a boy or girl begins to enter puberty, he or she becomes less comfortable with the physical closeness. The child will start backing away from kisses and hugs, feeling uncomfortable about the physical demonstration of affection.

This is a natural process resulting from the bodily changes that take place during puberty. With the production of hormones and the development of the secondary sex characteristics, the adolescent boy or girl begins to experience a surge of sexual desire and drive. The child begins to feel uncomfortable about being both emotionally and physically close to parents. The old incest taboo rears its head. This is Mother Nature's way of pushing the child out of the family as he or she begins seeking a peer who will ultimately, in some way, duplicate that original nurturing formula that was present in birth. Most adolescents and young adults look for a person with whom they can be both physically and emotionally close. The drive to experience intimacy in both a physical and an emotional way is a powerful force drawing people toward marriage and remarriage.

Emotional Maturity

Families either help or hinder young people as they try to grow up and take over their own lives. Some families help people mature, take responsibility, take charge of their own affairs. In these families, children have begun separating from their parents in a healthy way in childhood. They are people who, after completing high school, go out into the world, live alone for a period of time, and develop their own sense of individuality and adequacy. These people are ready to find a peer with whom they can become both physically and emotionally close and share the companionship of marriage. Such emotional maturity draws couples to the intensifying experience of intimacy.

Dynamics and Dimensions of Marriage

For most couples, the movement toward the wedding is not a casual meandering that brings them surprisingly and unwittingly to marriage. Rather, couples approaching a wedding do so intentionally. As they encounter each other in the relationship, a force builds and binds them increasingly together. By the time they reach the wedding, patterns have emerged in the tapestry of their lives together and the strands have been laced together into a network.

We have just examined some of the forces that bring couples to marry. We will now focus on the relationship that develops and explore some of the dimensions of marriage. Earlier we defined the premarital state; now we are going to define the marital state.

Marriage means many things to many people. It has been defined in thousands of ways. Philosophers have wrestled with its definition; sociologists have struggled to measure it; psychologists have tried to describe it; theologians have attempted to explain its meaning and purpose. Yet no one definition of marriage seems to do it justice. Perhaps that is because no definition by a single discipline encompasses all the dimensions of marriage. This could also be a way of saying that no matter how thoroughly it is described and defined, marriage has a mystery about it. This mystery may be what keeps any definition from being inclusive and total.

We are not going to attempt to define marriage comprehensively. Our purpose, rather, is to provide a working definition, one relevant for professionals working with couples in a prewedding counseling context. Our definition will be primarily relationship-oriented.

The Dimensions of Marriage

It seems to us that marriage can be best defined as multidimensional. In other words, we see marriage as a relationship that functions on many levels. We are not saying that marriage is the only relationship that is multidimensional. Other relationships also operate on more than one dimension, such as those between employer and employee, employee and employee, parent and child, and so forth. We are contending, however, that marriage is especially intricate in its intermingling of many dimensions. We want to look at some of the dimensions and describe them briefly, so that readers can sense the complexity of the marital relationship.

- Marriage has a social and companionship dimension, which means a special sharing in social and interpersonal activities, whether they be undertaken together or separately.
- Marriage has a geographical or spatial dimension, which means an uncommon sharing of space and physical proximity, whether the spouses do things together or apart.

- Marriage has an affectional and nurturing dimension, which means an intimate sharing of emotional and physical comfort that expresses caring and support.
- Marriage has a sexual or reproductive dimension, or both, which means a unique physical, sensual, reproductive, and sexual sharing.
- Marriage has a psychological dimension, which means a unique sharing of emotions and fantasies.
- Marriage has a cognitive and planning dimension, which means a special sharing as the spouses think about life, make plans, discuss goals, and carve out futures together.
- Marriage has a dimension of happiness and humor, and involves traditions that are part of the couple's unique bonding. Marital joy implies a perspective for dealing with crises that will inevitably confront the marriage.
- Marriage has a fiscal and financial nature, which means a particular kind of sharing not only in the accumulation of money, but also in its use and distribution.
- Marriage has a recreational and pleasure dimension, which means a remarkable kind of sharing in the replenishing and renewal that keep a relationship alive.
- Marriage has an existential and philosophical dimension, which means a specific sharing in regard to religious and spiritual attitudes, behaviors, and life values.
- Marriage has a legal status in our country, which means that the spouses incorporate their relationship into the civil and legal process of society.
- Marriage has a paradoxical dimension. We find couples and their variety of marital relationships fascinating. It intrigues us that there are some couples who, although they have a relationship that is indeed multidimensional, lack a legal dimension. In our society, we call them unmarried. There are other couples who, although they possess the legal dimension and are legally married, have been disengaging from each other in all of the dimensions just listed. Yet we call them married.

It seems to us that our society's nomenclature, from a psychological perspective, is upside-down. Given our definition, the uniqueness of marriage is its multidimensional character. It is likely, then, for a couple to be married already, psychologically speaking, before they possess a marriage license. It is also possible for a couple to have a legal marriage but not to be or ever to have been married psychologically.

The typical definition of marriage is too narrow and simplistic. If marriage is in fact multidimensional, then during the dating process, the tapestry is already being woven and the patterns are already emerging. By the time the couple reaches the wedding, the relationship is already operative on all levels, at least in some form, with the exception of the legal dimension. To say that the marriage begins with the wedding is inaccurate. We are suggesting, therefore, that it is more helpful for the premarital and remarital counselor to view the marriage as having begun before the wedding. The wedding announces what has already taken place on a more private plane. *Psychological marriage* precedes *legal marriage*.

The Impact of Bonding

We have been defining marriage as a multidimensional relationship that is unique in operating on many levels. Because we do not think this definition is totally encompassing, we would also like to suggest another definition of marriage that will run parallel to and enrich our definition of marriage as multidimensional.

We see marriage as having a unique kind of bonding, as being held together with a kind of glue. This glue can also be described as the couple's closeness and as their positive view of their relationship.[2] The multileveled connections that exist between a husband and wife feed into this bonding. These connections attract them initially and maintain the relationship on many levels. Other dimensions of the bonding cause the couple not only to weave their lives together, but also to find a power and satisfaction in that unique relationship.

Bonding and Dependency

One of the dimensions that feeds into the bonding process during the more serious stages of the dating relationship has to do with dependency needs. The possibilities that the potential mate provides in terms of fulfilling natural dependency needs is a powerful attracting force that impels people toward a marital relationship.

All people, no matter how healthy, have some dependency needs. Although there tends to be greater "stickiness" to the "glue" when exaggerated dependency needs exist, making the glue set more quickly and tightly, the counselor needs to understand that dependency needs factor into the bonding process for all human beings. The premarital counselor should not underestimate the degree to which the potential mate can bring necessary and appropriate psychological closeness. The desire for wholeness and togetherness—the desire to feel complete and close—helps people bond.

Bonding and Self-Esteem

Another ingredient that contributes to bonding is self-esteem. All people, regardless of their level of self-esteem, see the possibility of receiving from a marital partner feelings of worth and well-being. As in the case of dependency needs, it is often true that people with low self-esteem expect that their spouse will in some way make them feel whole, good, attractive, worthy, and wanted—in other words, that he or she will raise their self-esteem. These expectations, values, and dreams of what the other spouse can do are powerful attracting and maintaining forces in the marriage. To be liked, desired, and wanted is important for all people, regardless of where their self-esteem is on the continuum between healthy and unhealthy.

The Bonding Process

We have been suggesting that marriage is a unique interpersonal relationship. Not only are there strong, particular forces that draw individuals toward each other, but these forces function as a kind of gravitational force in the relationship. We are calling the attracting force and the gravitational force bonding. It is important to underscore the concept of bonding, because it is crucial for a counselor to understand that the marital relationship is rarely casual. The marital relationship is extremely intense for the majority of couples. We are trying to communicate that intensity with the words *bonding* and *glue*.

Bonding is already at work premaritally, drawing the couple together initially. It continues to hold the relationship together during marriage. We believe that the bonding process follows a particular progression in most relationships.[3] In a general way of speaking, we think of bonding as beginning privately in each individual during the dating relationship. At some point in time, each person in the relationship says on the inside, "That person is for me." The premarital counselor can usually establish with the help of each individual when that internal event occurred.

The second step in the bonding process is interactional. At some point after the first step has been taken, each person begins to indicate, verbally and nonverbally, that they hold the other person in special regard. This rarely takes place at one point or event, but is again a process. In some sense and in some way, each person says to the other, "You are for me." By this time, the couple is already deep in the bonding process and the relationship has already connected on many levels. Several dimensions of the union are already operative.

As the glue sets more and more firmly, the couple finally make the third step in the bonding process. As a last declaration, the couple announces to the world what has already happened to them privately and interactionally. When the couple announce their engagement and have the wedding, they are declaring that the bonding has already set. We think it very important for the premarital counselor to understand that almost always when the couple comes to premarital or remarital counseling, they are psychologically speaking, already married.

This brings us to a peculiar dilemma facing the counselor. Although we have suggested that the couple is already married by the time they approach the wedding—that the glue has already set in some sense—the couple may not see it that way. Although covertly the two may sense that they are in some ways especially locked together, on the overt level they still perceive themselves as unmarried. Society also supports the overt view; the couple is not yet married. This paradox presents the premarital counselor with a dilemma: whereas from the counselor's perspective the task is (in a sense) marital counseling, from the couple's perspective the task is premarital counseling.

∽

We have stressed that marriage, whether it be a first marriage or a remarriage, begins before the wedding. We maintain that the glue that binds a man and a woman together in marriage begins to thicken and set before the wedding comes along. Accepting these ideas will have an important impact on the manner in which the premarital or remarital counselor functions.

The counselor operating within a predominantly pathological framework or steeped in traditional therapeutic approaches often experiences difficulty in working with premarital and remarital couples. Such a counselor may still perceive marriage as beginning with the wedding and will then structure the counseling process on that assumption. Although some couples are still in the process of deciding whether to wed during premarital counseling, and even in remarital counseling, this is rarely true in the majority of cases. If the counselor adopts that mind-set, both the counselor and the couple will be exasperated with the counseling process, because they will be working in opposite directions.

We have been trying to communicate that marriage is not an accidental and casual event that individuals undergo. Rather, marriage originates in powerful forces that attract people to it. Couples look to marriage because they expect some kind of change or growth. The couple's attitude before the wedding is not that of people casually strolling toward an event, but rather that of people drawn headlong toward some crucial climax in their relationship. In the vernacular, this is described as being "head over heels in love."

Claude Guldner has accurately described the powerful way in which people in couples are attracted to each other.[4] He called the premarital state one of bliss. The attraction in a relationship is indeed intense, powerful, and often all-consuming. When one thinks for a moment about how some marriages can be so intense that they drive people to alcoholism, drug addiction, homicide, or suicide, it should not be surprising that the power that can drive people to extremes in marriage already exists prior to the wedding.

Unless the premarital counselor understands that couples are usually impelled toward marriage and are in search of growth, he or she may try to intervene, change, or stop that movement. We suspect that in most cases any attempt to do so will be unsuccessful, and that the forces are so powerful that the marriage will probably come about one way or another anyhow.

∽

In this chapter we have examined marriage as a multidimensional psychological process and as a legal event. We have shown that it is crucial for the counselor to clarify his or her own personal beliefs and attitudes about the premarital process and marriage itself in order to be effective in counseling with couples. On this foundation, in the next chapter we introduce the process of premarital and remarital counseling.

Part Two

The Counseling Process

Chapter Three

Foundations and Goals of Premarital and Remarital Counseling

With this chapter, we introduce a new section of the book. Part Two will develop a model for premarital counseling. It will focus on the couple counseling approach and examine structural and administrative issues in premarital and remarital counseling.

Contexts of Premarital Counseling

There are three main providers of premarital counseling: clergy, professional mental health workers, and physicians. Clergy provide the greatest amount of premarital and remarital counseling and education, either directly or through marriage education programs that they oversee.

We suspect that mental health counselors in agencies and clinics have been providing premarital and remarital counseling in greater numbers in recent years. This involvement has usually taken two forms. On the one hand, counselors have participated in premarital counseling programs sponsored by groups or institutions in the community. Their role has been primarily that of leader, presenter, or facilitator. On the other hand, unmarried couples experiencing more serious conflicts and deciding whether to marry have sought counselors to evaluate their relationship, especially when at least one partner has been married before.

Although physicians have been involved before the wedding with many couples down through the decades, the work of the physician in prewedding counseling has been rather specific.[1] Either the physician has been consulted to provide a premarital physical exam, or the doctor is consulted about contraception and family planning. It is true that physicians frequently see individuals before the wedding; however, they usually do not see couples together, nor do they focus on the relationship itself. Thus, although physicians may see a high number of individuals before their marriages, doctors' involvement is of a different nature from that of the other two groups of providers.

We believe that the context of premarital and remarital counseling is crucial in shaping both the methodology of the counseling and the expectations of the couple seeking counseling. We want to explore a variety of contexts, tracing the impact of each on client expectations and counseling methodology.

Parish Setting

Since a significant percentage of premarital and remarital counseling in this country is conducted in the local church in preparation for the wedding, we need to examine this setting in order to trace its impact. Our primary basis of knowledge and information about the practice of premarital and remarital counseling is the published literature. Similarly, our primary criterion for inclusion of information in this book is that it can be documented by reliable sources. Our review of the literature has shown that almost all that has been published in regard to premarital counseling in religious settings reports or refers to Christian church settings. Therefore our discussion focuses on Christian settings, but we do not intend to be exclusive, and we believe that much of what we present can be readily adapted to other religious settings. With this in mind, we shall explore a variety of expectations.

Denominational Expectations

Because we are a pluralistic nation, we have a large number of religions and religious denominations. Not only do these various religions and denominations have different traditions regarding doctrinal issues and religious or liturgical practices, but they also have a diversity of traditions regarding the role of the religious leader or pastor as premarital and remarital counselor.

In broad terms, the Christian religious tradition can be divided into large and somewhat distinct categories. On the one hand, there are denominations that view marriage as a sacrament. This sacramental orientation toward marriage gives a distinct responsibility to the clergy. The pastor is responsible for admitting candidates into all of the sacraments, of which marriage is only one. The sacramental responsibility has within it a kind of guardianship. It is important to understand, however, that this guardianship is not simply implied. These denominations are explicit in either their canon law or their constitutional statutes about the nature of marriage and about the characteristics and nature of the candidates to be admitted to marriage.

On the other hand, denominations that do not view marriage as a sacrament also have denominational expectations. Such Christian denominations place a high emphasis and value on marriage, and they explicitly and implicitly attempt to define not only the nature of marriage in a Christian sense but also the kind of preparation and characteristics that the couple needs to have for the Christian marriage to be consummated. Although the guardianship focus of these denominations is not clear, and seems subtle and diffused, we believe that it is nonetheless active.

In addition to the sacramental and nonsacramental denominational expectations, a third expectation cuts across all denominations. This we call a pastoral counseling expectation. Since the advent of the pastoral counseling movement and the deemphasis in pastoral ministry on the simply and explicitly religious or ritualistic, clergy have been expected, particularly through pastoral counseling courses in seminaries, to meet the personal and counseling needs of parishioners. By publishing handbooks on premarital counseling and literature for couples to read in preparation for their marriage, denominations encourage the idea that the pastor is to provide premarital counseling. Many churches or clergy require couples to complete premarital counseling or participation in a premarital education program. All of these expectations, then, collectively suggest that premarital counseling not only is important but also should be taken seriously by both clergy and premarital couples.

In addition to denominational and pastoral counseling expectations, we are seeing community expectations placed on premarital and remarital counseling. For instance, the Episcopal Church in America, led by Bishop George Reynolds of Tennessee and retired Bishop Edward McBurney of Illinois, has inspired the Community Marriage Policies. In various communities throughout the United States, clergy of many denominations have come together to approve a community policy regarding marriage preparation. The policies, signed by clergy in over thirty-two communities, such as Fresno, California; Fairbanks, Alaska; Beaver, Pennsylvania; and others, contains several points, including the following:

- Requiring a significant period of preparation, from three to six months
- Mandating at least two premarital counseling sessions in which a relational instrument or inventory is used
- Training married couples to serve as mentors and role models for those who are approaching marriage
- Teaching Biblical doctrines on morality, marriage, and divorce
- Encouraging engaged and married couples to participate in intensive weekend enrichment seminars
- Providing postnuptial support for already married couples

In Modesto, California, for example, some seventy-five church groups have come together to adopt a community marriage policy that includes a four-month waiting period, psychological personality profiles, and multiple sessions of conflict-resolution counseling for engaged couples.

Although we are dealing with denominational expectations that are part of premarital and remarital counseling in the parish setting, it is important to underscore that clergy and other religious leaders are not solely agents of their denomination. Each minister or religious leader is also licensed to perform and thus to ensure the legality of marriages. Ministers therefore carry a dual identity: pastor and civil agent. Although we are a country that prides itself on the separation of church and state, we specifically give clergy a responsibility to activate the contract and legalize the marriage on behalf of the state.

This dual responsibility causes many ministers to experience a constant state of tension. Pastors who perform a marriage as agents of the denomination will need to seek and approve of certain values, expectations, and characteristics in the couple. If, on the other hand, pastors perform weddings in the civil sense, the expectations and characteristics they seek in the couple might be quite different. The tension is enhanced when couples primarily want to have their relationship legalized and are not particularly interested in seeing it either as explicitly religious or as symbolizing or initiating their participation in active church life.

It would probably be a welcome relief if we could resolve this dilemma for clergy. We strongly believe, however, that there is no resolution to this dilemma as long as clergy have both responsibilities and certifications. Clergy who have difficulty with ambiguity or need to have their role and path clearly spelled out will no doubt experience tension. To resolve that tension, they will want to move in one direction or the other. They will either prefer to avoid marriages in which the couple does not meet denominational expectations regarding the religious nature of their behavior, or they will move in the other direction by giving up any kind of premarital counseling and performing all weddings. We would like to suggest, however, that tension is part of life. To resolve that tension in one direction or another might be easier, but we suspect that such a resolution would detract from the challenges, growth, and excitement of being in the ministry.

Congregational Expectations

Just as there is a diversity of traditions in denominational expectations, there are also varied traditions of premarital and remarital counseling in local congregations. In some congregations, premarital counseling has been a long-established tradition, begun by earlier pastors. In other congregations, premarital counseling, particularly remarital counseling, is either brief and superficial or hardly established at all. We suggest that it behooves the pastor to ascertain the local tradition.

If premarital counseling has been established in the congregation, the expectation that the pastor will not only see couples prior to the wedding but also conduct some specialized kind of educational counseling is already entrenched. In congregations in which the premarital counseling expectation is not present, the pastor attempting to introduce such counseling needs to be aware that it will not always be greeted with agreement. Many parishioners, especially in small towns and rural areas where people often already know each other too well and are greatly interested in privacy, shy away from any public exposure. They will often resist any move toward premarital counseling. Parishioners are likely to respond negatively not only because it is new and different, but also because they might perceive it as meddling. Before any minister attempts to introduce a broad program of premarital or remarital counseling, it is important to assess the congregational expectation. The minister will also need to lay the groundwork. There are some congregations in which premarital or remarital counseling might be difficult to establish; conceivably, there are congregations in which counseling should not be attempted.

Whether premarital and remarital counseling has been a tradition in the churches that pastors are serving, or whether they are establishing such a procedure for the first time, they should be sure to have the appropriate local church committee or board approve policies or guidelines about counseling. As congregations establish premarital and remarital counseling guidelines, they will articulate their expectations and thus help to make them explicit for members who will be seeking weddings in the church.

Couples' Expectations

Couples approaching premarital and remarital counseling are generally viewing their relationship as positive and are excitedly making plans for their future. This means that they are not approaching counseling with an orientation toward problems. They see their relationship not only as something that they want, but also as something that they need. They have a keen desire to be together and feel intense excitement and oneness. Although this may not characterize every couple, it certainly characterizes the majority. Their blissful state greatly affects their expectations of premarital and remarital counseling and the counseling process. Bliss leads couples to avoid negatives and focus on positives.

Influence of Expectations in Parish Setting

The variety of expectations in the parish setting will influence the methodology of the premarital and remarital pastoral counselor. If the pastor chooses to follow denominational expectations that prescribe a guardianship aspect to the pastoral function, his or her method of dealing with a couple will have distinct overtones of this guardianship orientation. Such a pastor will likely have a premarital and remarital counseling model that could be characterized as investigative and examining. The methodology, then, will be primarily constructed to discern whether the couple meets the institutional expectations. It will essentially place the institution and its desires over the couple and their desires.

In a similar fashion, the pastor who resolves the dilemma of the civil versus the religious responsibility in the direction of the religious will develop a methodology for premarital and remarital counseling that again will primarily attempt to discern whether the candidates meet the institutional expectations and ideals for the marital relationship.

On the other hand, a pastor influenced by the expectations of the pastoral counseling tradition will develop a methodology that is designed to place the couple in a more important position than the institution and its ideals or expectations. That methodology will have as its expectation an attempt to meet the people as they are, both in life and in their relationship.

All of this is complicated by the premarital or remarital couple's expectations. If it is true, as we believe, that premarital and remarital couples have essentially positive feelings about each other and their upcoming marriage, then the pastor using a screening agent model will frequently find the counseling sessions tense and difficult. The pastoral counselor using a developmental model to work with couples will be able, we believe, to deal more effectively with each couple as they are.

Clinics and Agencies

Social service agencies and counseling clinics are more ambiguous than the clergy about their expectations, frequently not defining them closely. Nonetheless, counseling agencies and clinics have subtle and implicit expectations regarding both the role of the counselor and the purpose of their program or therapy.

Theoretical Expectations

A counselor's theoretical framework will influence the premarital counseling methodology. We have already discussed how the individual psychotherapeutic theoretical framework influenced therapists in previous decades. This theoretical framework essentially failed to conceptualize marriage as a bilateral relationship. The focus on the individual rather than on interaction probably accounts for the fact that psychotherapists in the earlier half of the twentieth century rarely did premarital counseling.

We believe that an interactional and systemic theoretical framework also influences the methodology of a premarital and remarital counselor. The systemic framework implies an emphasis on the importance of relationships, motivating the therapist to be interested in and willing to work with premarital couples. The systemic theoretical model assumes that any change in the behavior or attitude of one person automatically changes the relationship. This theoretical framework thus motivates the counselor to be involved with premarital and remarital couples.

The theoretical framework also influences methodology in other ways. Because the clinician functioning within an interactional and systemic theoretical framework already values relationships, he or she will be motivated to see the couple together. With a theoretical framework that conceptualizes the relationship as visible only in the presence of both people, the premarital and remarital counselor making use of this framework will have his or her methodology influenced by it and will seek to have both parties present for the counseling sessions.

Couples' Expectations

Couples coming to counseling centers and social service agencies bring various expectations about the premarital and remarital counseling process. Couples seeking counseling before marriage can be divided into three categories: those with no real conflict or problems, those experiencing difficulty or conflict in the relationship, and those planning to remarry.

Couples who come for counseling before their first marriage and who present themselves as lacking premarital conflicts probably appear infrequently in the clinic population. Such couples probably participate more often in pastoral premarital counseling. In that sense, we could say that the couples clergy see are more commonly "normals." If such a couple comes to a clinic because the clinic has stressed its involvement in premarital or remarital counseling or provides a group program for premarital counseling, one could anticipate that they will have a positive outlook and that they will have not a problem-solving but a skill-enhancement orientation.

Couples who come more frequently to counseling centers for premarital and remarital counseling are experiencing difficulty in their relationship. The presence of conflict and tension means that they are interested in evaluating their relationship and attempting either to understand the nature of the conflict or to make some decision about their future together. Thus, these couples frequently expect something different from the "normals." The expectations of these clients more closely approximates the expectations of those who undergo couple therapy. We therefore suggest that the premarital counselor follow a model more influenced by couple therapy. The model we outline later will also provide a good base for working with the couple experiencing conflict.

The third type of couple who comes to a counseling center is planning remarriage, whether to the same person or to a different person. These couples frequently include people who have had previous couple therapy. Such people come with an expectation that the remarital counselor will evaluate the relationship. They are specifically concerned with determining whether patterns that were present in the previous relationship exist in the current one.

Medical Setting

Couples who see a physician before marrying also expect certain things from the medical visit and examination. They generally expect to obtain birth control information and sexual information during the consultation. They rarely expect the physician to become involved in their interpersonal dynamics, unless there is some conflict regarding birth control or sex.

The nature of medical practice also influences the premarital consultation. Patients perceive the physician as knowledgeable about reproductive and sexual functioning and contraception and seek out the physician before the wedding specifically because of these areas of expertise. In addition, a doctor's characteristically high patient volume limits the consultation time significantly. With some exceptions, physicians simply cannot spend five to ten hours with premarital couples. This is compounded by the fact that physicians, and medicine in general, are still primarily individual-oriented and see only individuals in prewedding consultations. Few physicians, apparently, have moved toward seeing couples together.

Format for Premarital and Remarital Counseling

One of the issues that each premarital and remarital counselor needs to settle is whether the counseling is going to be individual, concurrent, conjoint, or some combination of all three. The format of counseling and therapy has evolved. In the beginning of the psychotherapeutic movement, the one-to-one relationship was sacred. No therapist would have seen the spouse of a patient being treated in psychotherapy. In the second stage of the evolutionary process, the therapist saw both spouses, but separately. This process, called concurrent psychotherapy, came into prominence as therapists became interested in interactional as well as intrapsychic aspects. The third stage, seeing the couple together from the very beginning, was called conjoint couple counseling. The conjoint model uses the conjoint format exclusively. This format developed as therapists became more interested in interactional than intrapsychic processes or dynamics.

Like psychotherapy, education evolved. Although education significantly predates therapy, the process of development was rather similar. In the twelfth through the sixteenth centuries in Europe, education was primarily given on a tutorial basis. The relationship of the student to the master was like an apprenticeship. Again, the one-to-one relationship was valued and respected. However, as the demand for education increased, the tutorial process slowly gave way to a class format. Prior to the seventeenth century, the class format was practiced, although all age ranges were present in the class. Today we would refer to that as ungraded education. In the seventeenth century, education moved to a third step—graded education, and people were separated into classes by ages.

As mentioned earlier, there is sparse literature on the development of premarital counseling. As best as we can determine, prewedding sessions followed the same evolution as education and psychotherapy in terms of format. In the few references that are available, it appears that premarital counseling was first done on an individual basis, then in a concurrent format, then in both a concurrent and a conjoint format, and finally in an exclusively conjoint format.[2]

In our experience, the conjoint premarital and remarital counseling model is the most productive. We encourage its use for a number of reasons. First, the conjoint format implicitly suggests to couples that the counselor values not only the individual persons, but also the relationship. Second, the format allows the counselor to see how the couple interacts and to observe the relationship. Third, by seeing both people together, the counselor heightens the bilateralism of the relationship. Bilateralism means that marriage is a two-way street, a quid pro quo experience. Education that is one-sided, or unilateral, is unproductive and ineffective because marriage is not one-sided. Clinical observation and research have shown that relationships achieve the most growth when the effort put into the relationship is two-sided. Fourth, using the conjoint couple format also underscores that the counselor does not want to be the keeper of secrets, which the concurrent format allows. If one member of the couple is not ready to deal with something in the presence of the other, the counselor's private knowledge of secrets will not help the couple work out their problems.

Goals of Premarital and Remarital Counseling

The design for the conjoint premarital and remarital counseling model sets out to accomplish several different goals. We discuss seven of those goals here.

1. *Clarification of self.* In the premarital and remarital counseling process, each partner establishes an "I" position. The process is designed to help each person sketch out thoughts, feelings, beliefs, and fantasies. By the time the sessions have come to a close, each person's identity will have become clearer to all those involved.

2. *Clarification of other.* As the counseling process helps to clarify each person in terms of thoughts, feelings, beliefs, and fantasies, the partner gains a clearer picture of the person with whom they are in a relationship and whom they are going to marry. Each person gains a clearer picture of the uniqueness of the other's personality.

3. *Binding anxiety.* Couples moving toward the wedding are frequently anxious. The anxiety arises from a variety of sources. Couples are anxious for the wedding to go smoothly and pleasantly. But there is another kind of anxiety, one related to the relationship itself. Couples worry whether it will work, whether it will turn out like their parents' marriages. By taking an ordered and methodical look at the relationship, the premarital and remarital counseling process will give the couple a sense of the nature of the relationship and some skills necessary to aid its continuing growth and development. In pastoral counseling sessions, the couple will also come to understand some of the basic mechanics of the wedding, which will help to relieve wedding anxiety.

4. *Building adventure.* A premarital or remarital counseling process will lead a couple into an adventure as it explores not only the nature of a couple's relationship but also the kinds of models their parents devised for marriage. If the counselor sets an inquisitive stance and is fascinated with the varieties of premarital relationships, he or she can instill in the couple a sense of excitement, adventure, and anticipation about the manner in which their relationship will grow and develop.

5. *Communication.* As another goal, the prewedding counseling process aims to improve communication. This occurs in a twofold way. First, the counseling process itself will help each person become more aware of his or her own thoughts, feelings, and actions. As such, the process will teach the man and woman to communicate their separate identities more effectively. Second, the counseling process will introduce the couple to or remind them of a special kind of language—the unique language of relationships (examples are discussed in Chapter Nine).

6. *Observation and prediction.* Part of the prewedding counseling process includes making observations about patterns or dynamics in the relationship that could cause difficulty or conflict. The prediction and feedback process is very important for couples. It serves as a warning light, so that if difficulty in the predicted area does develop, the couple has a way of interpreting its value and meaning. The prediction also takes the sting of surprise out of the conflict.

7. *Overcoming inhibitions.* One of the underlying and perhaps most important roles of premarital and remarital counseling is to

help the couple talk about specific areas of their relationship that they had not or could not talk about before. The counseling methodology we employ is specifically designed to address topics that couples have not previously considered together.

Goals such as these are important and help the premarital and remarital counselor apply a facilitative approach to the counseling process. Some counselors will find it valuable to present these goals to clients during the first session. These aims can be used as outcome goals in the counseling process. For example, at the beginning of each session, the premarital or remarital counselor could review the goals from the previous sessions and those of the current and future sessions. Recommending the use of these goals in the counseling session indicates our bias, of course. It suggests that although the premarital and remarital counseling process as we see it is therapeutic, education is one of its important ingredients.

Administrative Issues

We now want to discuss three important managerial issues that the counselor must face: the number and length of counseling sessions, the fees, and the use of printed materials.

The Number and Length of Sessions

The premarital and remarital counselor needs to make some decisions regarding the structure of the sessions, especially about the length and the number of sessions. In regard to the length of the sessions, we have found that premarital or remarital counseling is generally delivered in sessions that last one-and-a-half to two hours, whereas couple therapy is typically an hour. We recommend two hours per session for both premarital and remarital counseling.

In regard to the number of sessions, we suggest at least four to six two-hour sessions for nonclergy. This should be an adequate time for most couples to accomplish the material we are outlining. Because clergy need to include theological and wedding material, we suggest that they conduct an additional two-hour session.

Although we suggest a specific number of sessions, we are cognizant that couples have relationships of various lengths and differing histories. The time frame we have outlined is adequate for the couple whose premarital relationship is not more than three years old and whose families of origin are not terribly complex; that is, those that do not include a variety of marriages, many children, or a jumble of events. There are always exceptions, however, and the time frame will need to be modified to fit such couples. In the beginning of the first session, the counselor should determine the length of the premarital courtship. If it exceeds three years, the rule of thumb can be altered. We also suggest that in that preliminary session, the counselor articulate a plan with the couples, indicating the number of sessions and the general purpose of each unit, reminding the couple that this may have to be revised as the counseling process proceeds.

Fees

The setting has something to do with whether or not fees are charged for premarital counseling. Those in clinic settings will no doubt use the counseling fee schedule established by the agency in which they are working. The counselor in that setting, then, will need to discuss the fee with the premarital or remarital couple as with any other client.

For clergy, the issue of fees is more complex because there are often fees for the use of the building and the support of staff involved in the wedding. Then there is the issue of whether there is a fee for the pastor's time in premarital or remarital counseling. Historically, clergy have not required a fee for their time, especially when one member of the couple belongs to the congregation. While the couple has rarely been discouraged from giving a stipend, no fee was clearly established in advance.

More recently, however, with clergy spending significant hours in the counseling sessions, the added cost of the use of a premarital inventory, the rehearsal, the groom's dinner, the wedding service itself, and the reception, many pastors and congregations have established a fee for the premarital counseling ranging from $50 to $200. Sometimes this fee is clearly earmarked for the continuing education of the pastor, or it may be considered supplemental income.

Another area for decision making is fee setting with the appropriate board or committee for the use of the sanctuary, the organist, the janitor, and other related services. By establishing clear fee guidelines, pastors do not have to risk angering support staff when couples fail to give a stipend or give an exceedingly small one. In addition, with the press of weddings in many churches, particularly churches with "beautiful sanctuaries" that nonmembers often seek out, many congregations have established a reservation fee to prevent weddings from being canceled at the last minute or to avoid the scheduling conflicts caused when people schedule weddings impulsively rather than seriously.

Regardless of whether a congregation chooses to charge for the counseling process and other services, the policy should be clearly articulated in the prewedding manual that the church prepares and supplies to couples planning a wedding. As pastors struggle with the issue of fees, it is important for them to consider that the average cost of a wedding is currently about $25,000 by the time all aspects are included. It hardly seems inappropriate to charge $50 to $200 for the relationship counseling itself. If marriage is indeed important, then some investment is appropriate.

Use of Printed Materials

The premarital and remarital counseling process is often accompanied by the use of books, pamphlets, and other material. If the counselor wants to use resources in the counseling process (bibliotherapy), he or she should devote time and attention to selecting the material. The counselor also needs to determine whether the institution is going to supply these materials at no charge or whether the couple must purchase them.

As mentioned earlier, clergy are encouraged to develop a brochure or booklet describing the nature of the premarital and remarital counseling sessions, the details of the wedding mechanics in the given church, fees, and so forth. This booklet, widely distributed in the congregation, will help set an expectation about the counseling process and will disseminate the necessary information.

∽

In this chapter we have discussed the essential elements of the process of premarital and remarital counseling in religious, mental health, and medical settings. The counselor must consider a variety of approaches to the counseling process and the implications of each in regard to the goals to be achieved. In the next chapter we first outline our conjoint counseling model for premarital and remarital counseling, and then present the Dynamic Relationship History as a means to begin the counseling process.

Chapter Four

Conjoint Counseling and the Dynamic Relationship History

The premarital or remarital couple and the counselor approach each counseling session with a myriad of expectations and feelings. Before marriage, couples are beset with many emotions. There is the bliss, the happiness they have found in each other and the relationship. There is a sense of unreality: "Is this really happening to me?" In the midst of the joy and the happiness is a strange sense of wondering, "How did I get here?" Filled with such questions, anxious about the wedding and the future of their relationship, the couple approaches the counseling sessions. By the same token, the premarital and remarital counselor also has myriad expectations and feelings. As he or she looks at the couple, the counselor wonders, "What can I do, given their experience of the moment? Where do I begin? What can I do that will be of optimal help at this point in their lives?"

In our clinical experience we have found that both the couple and the counselor are often confused about the other party's role, expectations, and goals. The couple and counselor are thrown together at a time when neither may be quite sure where to go or in what direction to move.

This chapter has a dual purpose: (1) to present a conjoint premarital and remarital counseling model that will give the couple an opportunity to look at their relationship, to expand their thinking about their relationship and their lives together, and to begin a process that they hope will continue in the future; and (2) to detail for the premarital and remarital counselor a methodology that will provide both a sense of direction and an understanding of the appropriate depths of the process.

A Design for Conjoint Couple Counseling

In this chapter, we sketch an overall design for our conjoint couple premarital and remarital counseling model. The parts of the model are not typically accomplished in one counseling session but may encompass several sessions. The following outline is suggested:

Part 1: Introduction. During the first session, the counselor spends time becoming acquainted with the couple and their counseling goals and expectations.

Part 2: Dynamic Relationship History (DRH). Also during the first session, the counselor evaluates the couple's relationship.

Part 3: Family-of-Origin Exploration (FOE). The counselor examines the nature and characteristics of the partners' families of origin. This exploration, which is a search for the parental models for marriage, will be described in Chapter Five.

Part 3a: Parents Attend a Session (Optional). This segment is an alternate conclusion to Part 3. It consists of inviting the parents of the bride and groom into the session to say good-bye to their children, to welcome the new couple into the family, and to allow the parents to pass on familial wisdom.

Part 4: Premarital Inventory. This part of the design begins early, usually during the first session, when the counselor presents the rationale for and has the couple take a comprehensive premarital or remarital inventory. Information from the inventory is used throughout the sessions as a basis for feedback, discussion, and skill building in areas such as communication, decision making, conflict resolution, budgeting, and so forth.

Part 5: Wedding Preparation. This portion, in which the counselor explains the mechanics of the wedding and theology, is performed only by clergy.

Part 6: Postwedding Session (Bonus). In this counseling session, scheduled six months after the wedding, the counselor can check in and check up with the couple to support the premarital counseling.

Part 1: Introduction

The premarital and remarital counselor may or may not have any previous knowledge of the couple. Although clergy, more frequently than nonclergy counselors, may know one or both parties well, it is nonetheless important for the counselor to spend some time at the beginning of the first counseling session becoming familiar with the couple and establishing a positive relationship with them. In spite of a general knowledge of the couple as individuals, the counselor will rarely have specific knowledge about their relationship.

Getting Acquainted

We believe that the counselor should spend the opening minutes of the first session finding out the basics of the relationship. This is particularly necessary if the premarital or remarital counselor does not know one or both of the people to be married.

In the introduction, the counselor should determine the basics: names, ages, parents, employment, educational background, length of time of the dating relationship, the wedding date, and so on. Some premarital and remarital counselors find it helpful to use a printed inventory or questionnaire that can provide the basic information about the couple. In addition, clergy may want to gather details about the wedding at this time, via a printed information sheet.

Explanation of the Counseling Process

After the counselor has become acquainted with the couple and has obtained basic information, he or she can begin to discuss the counseling process itself. We suggest that the counselor first introduce Part 2, the Dynamic Relationship History (DRH). The counselor can briefly describe the nature of the DRH by simply informing the couple that it is a historical view of their relationship, beginning with the time they first met each other, continuing up to the present, and including the wedding.

The couple may wonder why the counselor wants to explore and discuss their relationship history. They may be resistant to or even somewhat defensive about the process unless an appropriate explanation is made. Therefore we suggest that the counselor supply the couple with the following rationale about the DRH process. First, the DRH provides the counselor with a methodology for becoming acquainted with the couple, for getting to know who they are as individuals. Second, it gives the counselor an opportunity to review with the couple where they have been together and what kinds of experiences and events have influenced their lives. Third, the DRH will give the counselor and couple an opportunity to look at the patterns they have established in their relationship. By taking the opportunity to look at these, the couple will gain not only some awareness of their relationship, but also an opportunity to change things that they want to change for future growth and happiness.

Premarital Inventory

Since there is not a separate inventory for remarital couples, here we use the term *premarital inventory* to include remarital issues and topics included in the comprehensive premarital inventories.

After the counselor has become acquainted with the couple and has explained the DRH, he or she should introduce the couple to the specific inventory or other assessment devices chosen for the sessions. The counselor should briefly explain the instrument or instruments and give specific instructions about completing the inventory.

Premarital and remarital counselors using inventories will need to allow extra time between the first sessions for the couple to complete the inventories and for the counselor to score them and study the results. With an inventory such as PREPARE, which is sent away for scoring, it takes eight to ten days for the results to be returned. Some inventories, such as FOCCUS, which can be hand-scored, can be available sooner, although the counselor still needs to allow time to score and study the results.

Some premarital counselors prefer to limit the first session to administrative details, simply getting acquainted, explaining the DRH, administering the inventory, and discussing the contract. If this method is employed, then the DRH and the evaluation of the relationship will not begin until the second session. The counselor may then need to make some adjustment in regard to the total number of counseling sessions.

Deciding the Number of Sessions

We mentioned earlier that the number of sessions in a premarital and remarital counseling process can, for most couples, be determined in advance. Nonetheless, we think it important that after the counselor receives the basic information about the lengths of the courtship and DRH, he or she can decide with the couple how many sessions it will take to complete the work. If unusual situations exist or emerge in the relationship, the counselor can adjust the number of sessions.

For premarital and remarital counselors working outside the parish setting, we suggest five to seven two-hour sessions. Since the nonclergy do not need to include the wedding material of Part 5, they can spend the first session on Parts 1 and 2, namely, getting acquainted, covering the administrative basics, and beginning the DRH. Counselors can devote the next sessions to Parts 3 and 4. For example, in one session, they can finish the DRH and discuss families of origin. In the remaining two or three sessions, they can talk about such topics as communication, conflict resolution, intimacy, budgeting, and so forth. The last session is the wrap-up. The counselor can greatly enhance these last two or three sessions by weaving in information from the inventories administered earlier. Part 3a would add a sixth two-hour session. Part 6 would bring the total number of counseling sessions to between six and eight.

For clergy in parish settings, we suggest a minimum of six sessions. This process would include the sessions just outlined plus a session for the mechanics of the wedding, theological issues, and so forth. Including Part 3a or Part 6 would add one session each to the total number of counseling sessions.

With clergy counseling premarital and remarital couples, the central question in the couples' minds will be, "Will this pastor perform the wedding for us?" Premarital and remarital counseling will be more effective for the couple if the pastor agrees to perform the wedding for them, providing they participate in the counseling sessions.

Part 2: Dynamic Relationship History

We are defining the DRH as a structured way of looking at a relationship's history from the time the couple first met up to the wedding. It is like a social history, with some significant differences. The DRH is informational in its orientation. The process is that of discovering some of the basic events, dates, dating maneuvers, and conflicts in the premarital process. The purpose is to help the couple become aware of how they behave with each other, how they affect each other, and what patterns they have already established. The DRH is a structured initial interview applied exclusively to the premarital or remarital relationship.[1]

Before we move directly into DRH's methodology, we want to remind the premarital and remarital counselor again of the powerful forces that impel the couple toward each other and toward marriage, and of the fact that the couple, psychologically speaking, is already married. It is important to accept the relationship as it is and to go from there. The counselor's task as he or she uses the DRH is thus not only to take the people as they are but also to expand their understanding of the relationship.

With the DRH, the counselor can accomplish several tasks: help the couple gain some awareness of the dynamics and patterns of their relationship, give them some skills and tools for future growth, predict the type of crises or conflicts that might develop, and establish the possibility of future growth through enrichment and counseling experiences.

Premarital and remarital counseling is not to be conceived of as a process that can instill in the couple all they need to prevent any future conflict or even divorce. Not only would that be an impossible task but such an expectation would also be debilitating and constricting rather than enhancing and positive.

We like to think of premarital and remarital counseling in metaphorical terms, conceiving of the couple's relationship as the coming together of two rivers. The counselor is putting a canoe in the river at some point past the junction. To resist the existence of a relationship, in view of the force present in the river, would mean canoeing upstream. That is a difficult task at best. We visualize the counseling process instead as an attempt to influence the river's course.

Earlier in this chapter, we discussed the rationale for the DRH that the counselor might explain to the couple. We are now going to discuss the rationale from the counselor's perspective, providing a more extensive basis for the use of this methodology.

First, the DRH is a way of *structuring information* that is useful to both the couple and the counselor. The DRH not only will help the couple look at what is happening presently in their relationship, but also will aid them in making sense out of their past. The DRH's methodology will clarify and organize the patterns and dynamics in the relationship.

Second, the DRH *heightens an awareness of patterns.* The process enables the counselor and the couple to become aware of the couple interactional patterns and therefore to recognize and understand their impact more fully.

Third, the DRH *creates a sense of movement in the couple's lives.* By looking at their past while in a reflective setting, the couple can gain some perspective on how they started out single, entered into a relationship, and finally moved toward marriage.

Fourth, the DRH *involves the couple in the process on their own level.* People perceive relationships in very concrete terms. The DRH is designed to examine the relationship's dynamics in the manner in which the couple looks at it. With other methodologies, counselors often speak a language that couples do not understand and have such a different perspective that couples cannot get in touch with the process.

Fifth, the DRH *becomes a model for interaction,* because the counselor must do significant questioning. Because couples have frequently roped off certain areas from discussion, and because questioning is often taken as an attack or criticism, they find questioning in and of itself difficult. By using the DRH, the counselor models questioning for the couple, giving them some sense of the information and processes for obtaining it that one needs in order to understand another person.

The dating process can be obscuring in a certain way. Couples rope off and stop discussing certain areas. It often seems safer for them to steer clear of loaded topics. For example, the woman does not ask how much the man really drinks, and he does not ask how frequently she becomes sullen or silent for days on end. Questioning has an underlying risk in intimate relationships: it may open up conflict and negativity, which can dampen the relationship. Thus, in an effort to maintain the peace, promote the relationship, and avoid moving into dangerous water, couples tend not to question each other.

The questioning style of the DRH is intended to accomplish two tasks with couples. First, active questioning is meant to expand a couple's awareness. The questions help the couple become conscious of events or behaviors that they have taken for granted and have not looked at closely. Second, questions should expand the couple's thinking process. The questioning style therefore helps the couple to look at events and behaviors differently and to think "unthinkable thoughts" about what is happening in their lives. The primary purpose of the questioning style is to enlarge the couple's thought framework and their awareness of the relationship.

We want to underscore that the goal of the DRH is not to resolve all the couple's problems or conflicts so that they can move into the future without difficulties or fear of divorce. The purpose of the DRH is to help the couple open up, to get them to think and talk about what they have not been able to talk about, especially after they leave the counselor. Although this may seem to be an overstatement, we believe that what happens to the couple after they leave a session is often more important than what happens during the session.

The DRH is intended to help the couple take responsibility for their individual lives, for their life together, and for the joys and problems they create. In a sense, the value of the DRH is that it *serves as a milestone.* With the DRH, the counselor in a subtle but implicit way helps the couple see that they are no longer children. The couple can no longer blame parents or anyone else for their lives. From now on they must take responsibility for themselves if they are going to continue to grow and enjoy the relationship. For the counselor to resolve whatever disagreements may exist between the partners would be to do what their parents did for them when they were children. The task of the counselor is not to be a parent, but to promote the passage from childhood to adulthood, to encourage responsibility.

When working with a remarital couple in which one or both of the partners have been married before, the remarital counselor should conduct the DRH on the current relationship first. After concluding the DRH, it would be appropriate to conduct a brief DRH on the previous marriage or marriages. If the counselor focuses on an earlier relationship first, the couple will often receive it negatively. In addition, when the counselor has completed the DRH on the current relationship, he or she will have an idea of the kinds of unresolved themes that might appear in the brief DRH on any previous marriages.

When conducting a DRH on a previous relationship, the counselor should not go into as much detail as for the current relationship. For example, in surveying the three-year period before the birth of the first child, the counselor might simply ask the partner about conflictual issues during that time, rather than taking each of the three years separately, as would be done with the current relationship DRH. The more the counselor uses the DRH, the easier it will be to condense the DRHs of any previous relationships and yet find unresolved themes that the client has brought into the current relationship.

DRH Techniques

The DRH is a chronological exploration of the relationship. In our work with premarital and remarital couples, we have discovered that using a blackboard or newsprint can be important in the DRH. With a visual time line, the couple can more concretely visualize the movement of their relationship.

A blackboard can be easily erased, so dates, places, and events can be corrected as the couple moves along in their exploration of the relationship. The disadvantage of a blackboard is that once the material is erased, it is no longer available unless it is placed back on the board. With newsprint, the material is available because the counselor can retain the newsprint and time line.

In training people for premarital and remarital counseling, we have discovered that a few DRH techniques can help the counseling process. First, it is important for the counselor to write down what is being said rather than interpretations of it. Second, we suggest that the counselor write the events or happenings on the board or newsprint in simple, short, representative words or sentences that are large enough to read from a distance.

Whenever the counselor places dates and events on the time line, it is most efficient for him or her to stand or move around while writing on the newsprint or blackboard. The counselor's being on his or her feet sets a more informal tone for the sessions, which will help the couple feel more comfortable. At the same time, in a subtle way, the counselor's standing up establishes a definite sense that he or she is directing the session, which is reassuring to the couple.

We suggest that the counselor use a "Y" graph placed on a horizontal dimension for diagramming the DRH. (See Figure 4.1.) The graph allows for an exploration, and charting on a time line, of the individual lives of the couple before they came together. The dates and events of the relationship should be plotted clearly and distinctly along the time line as the premarital counselor covers the dating history.

We are not so much interested in the dates and events as we are in the patterns that are evolving and being established in the process. While we use the events and dates to frame the happenings of the relationship, our real interest is in exploring the manner in which John affects Mary and Mary affects John and how they begin to develop a particular pattern in their relating style.

Dyadic Questioning

Before we look at the specific questions used in the DRH, it is important to introduce the reader to a specific technique in our questioning process: dyadic questioning. In this process, the premarital and remarital counselor asks one partner questions about the other partner, especially when the counselor wants to elicit information (thoughts, feelings, beliefs, ideas, or fantasies) about nodal aspects of the couple's relationship. The information could be about the psychological aspects of their relationship or interpretive aspects of their history together. By asking one partner about the other partner's behavior, attitudes, or emotions, the counselor not only forces the couple to expand their thinking processes about their relationship, but also places the counselor in a meta-position to the couple. This dyadic questioning style keeps the focus systemic and makes the couple think rationally. The DRH, which is conducted with large dosages of dyadic questioning, impels the couple to fit together pieces of their own puzzle. This con-

Figure 4.1. DRH Couple Time Line
for John and Mary.

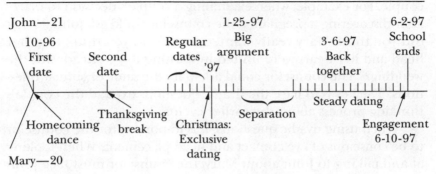

stant feedback into the couple's system pushes the couple to explore their complex relationship and their perceptions of the relationship.

When using dyadic questioning, the premarital and remarital counselor should bear in mind that there are three significant areas of focus for the dyadic questions.

First, some questions are targeted at eliciting feedback about *similarity and dissimilarity.* In other words, the dyadic questions are aimed at gathering information about the degree to which the partners are similar or dissimilar to each other. Many couples evolve a mythology that says that they are very different from each other, when to the outside observer it appears that the couple operates on very similar psychological levels, such as maturity, self-esteem, and so forth. A counselor can say something like the following when exploring the first date: "Mary, when you got back to your dormitory room and your roommate said to you, 'How did you like John?', what did you say?" Or, "How was John different from the other guys you dated?"

The second type of question aims to gather specific information about *couple interaction.* For example, if during the early dating period John became angry with Mary for dating another guy, ask Mary, "How did you explain John's anger? What did you think it was about? What was he wanting you to do? What did he do with his anger?" Then ask John, "What was Mary up to? How did you explain it to yourself? What was she trying to say to you?"

The third type of question aims to elicit further information about *nodal events* or *historical hiccups* that caused conflict for the couple. For example, when examining a couple's decision to marry after discovering a pregnancy, the counselor could ask John, "What did you think Mary really wanted to do? Do you think that her head and her heart were united in wanting to go ahead with the wedding?" The counselor could ask Mary the same or similar questions. The key is to have the dyadic questions expand the couple's thinking process about the earlier events.

When using dyadic questions, it is important for the counselor to be conscious of eye contact and head placement. When looking at and talking to John about Mary, the counselor must face John fully, or Mary will likely interrupt the process. Nonverbal focus is key to the successful use of the dyadic questioning process.

There are two types of questioning styles to use when exploring nodal events. The counselor puts *directive questions* to one of the partners because the counselor either wants to balance the interaction and have the more quiet partner talk, or desires specific information from one partner. *Nondirective questions* are directed to either partner. When using nondirective questions, the counselor should look between the couple or away from them entirely so as not to give some subtle clue as to which partner should speak first. This form of questioning is for the purpose of seeing which partner will initiate the response. Nondirective questioning allows the counselor to infer the relationship's structure and power distribution.

Questions Used in the DRH

Many of the questions in this chapter are written in a straight form, as if directed to each partner. It is very difficult to write entirely in the dyadic questioning style, partly because the DRH requires a focus that alternates between *nodal events* that need to be explored and *interactional processes* that need to be discovered. But do not let the monadic style of some of the questions mislead you—use the dyadic questioning style as much as possible. The counselor goes to the board or newsprint and asks the following questions:

First Meeting

- "When did the two of you meet? What year was it? How old were each of you at that time?"

- "How did you first meet? Did you know who the other one was before you met? Who introduced you? What do you remember about your first meeting?"

First Impressions

- "After you got back from your first date, if you had a best friend to whom you would have told everything, and he or she had said, 'What did you think of John/Mary?' what would you have said?" (Here is an excellent place to use dyadic questioning.)
- "What did you like about John/Mary?" (Ask each person this question about the other, using dyadic questioning.)
- "What attracted you to her/him? In what ways did you think you were similar?"
- "What did you discover about John/Mary that was different, unusual, or strange?"

Second Date

- "How long after the first meeting or date did the second date occur?"
- "Who initiated it?"
- "Where did you go and how did you decide what you were going to do on the date?"

Second Impressions

- "At the end of the second date, what did you find attractive about the other person?" (Use dyadic questions: "Mary, what do you think John found attractive about you?")
- "Did you discover anything else that was unusual, different, or strange?"

Family's and Friends' Responses

- "How did your friends respond to your dating the other person? What did they like about him/her? What didn't they like about the other person?"

Exclusivity and Inclusivity

- "Did you continue to date others? Was the dating of others discussed?"

- "When did you decide to stop dating others? If you stopped dating others without discussing it, when did you begin to know or sense that the other person was no longer interested in other people?"
- "If you discussed and decided not to date other people, how did this discussion go? When did it occur?"

Bonding Process: Steady Dating

- "When did each of you see yourself as going together or as 'going steady'?" (Remember to use dyadic questioning.)
- "How did you arrive at the decision? Did you discuss it or did it just happen?"
- "What did your friends think of your commitment to go steady? What did your parents think about your decision to go steady?"
- "When did you say to yourself 'He/she is for me!' or 'He/she is someone I'd marry'?" (Note: this is the point of internal commitment or psychological marriage.)

Separations

- "When the two of you went your separate ways for the summer, what did you say about the relationship? John, where did you think Mary was in regard to the relationship? Mary, where did you think John was in regard to the relationship? How would you each have defined the relationship at this point in time?" (Use dyadic questions.)

Bonding Process

- "When did you begin to say to the other, 'You're for me,' or 'I could see our getting married,' or 'I'd like to be with you forever,' or 'I could see myself marrying you'?" (Note: this is the point of external commitment.)

Engagement

- "Did you discuss getting engaged? Was it a surprise? When did you become engaged? Did you tell others? Did you make a public announcement?"

- "How did your parents react to the engagement? Did you inform them or request their permission?"

Conflict

- "During this time did you have any arguments?"
- "How often did you argue? What issues or concerns caused arguments?"
- "How did you make sense out of those arguments? How were the arguments resolved?"
- "Who initiated the peacemaking or making-up effort?"
- "What was the relationship like after you made up?"

Communication Behaviors

- "How did you know, Mary, if you said or did something John didn't like?" (Remember to use dyadic questioning.)
- "How did you know, John, if you said or did something Mary didn't like?"
- "How did you know, Mary, if you said or did something that pleased John?"
- "How did you know, John, if you said or did something that pleased Mary?"

Family-of-Origin Material

- "Mary, in what way does John handle anger like his father does?"
- "In what way, Mary, does John handle anger like his mother does?"
- "John, in what way does Mary handle anger like her father does?" (The counselor will continue similar dyadic questioning on other issues such as affection, money, leisure time, and so forth.)

Affection and Sex

- "How did you know Mary/John was happy with something you said or did? Did he/she tell you?"
- "When in the dating/courtship/engagement process did you become openly affectionate? Who initiated it?"

- "Have you become sexually involved as a couple? Did you discuss it first? What was your reaction to it?"
- "What differences do you see between affection and sex?"

Reaction to Engagement

- "What was your family's reaction to your engagement?"
- "Mary, how did you see John's father (and in another question, mother) reacting to the engagement?"
- "John, how did you see Mary's mother (and in another question, father) reacting to the engagement?"

Planning the Wedding

- "John, how do you see Mary's mother's involvement in planning the wedding? How about Mary's father's involvement?" (Remember the movie *The Father of the Bride!*)
- "Are there any problems with the wedding plans? To what extent are you as a couple involved in the wedding plans?"

Topical Areas and Issues of Focus

We have already indicated the general idea of the DRH—to explore the relationship from the time the couple first met until the present. We now want to outline briefly some of the areas of focus and the kinds of questions we ask, to give the premarital and remarital counselor a larger sense of what we do and what we are looking for. We also want to make it clear that the DRH involves moving through the history of the relationship in a month-by-month fashion. Unless the couple has an extensive dating history, the counselor usually has no difficulty accomplishing this task in the time frame indicated.

If you are using an assessment device such as PREPARE, PREPARE-MC, or FOCCUS, the inventory could also provide you with supplemental background information and scores that you may wish to validate or incorporate into some questions while you are conducting the DRH. The actual interpretation of inventory information or results usually follows the completion of the DRH.

There are a number of other issues to which the premarital and remarital counselor must attend, issues that do not necessarily emerge chronologically but rather have a thematic or topical flavor. The counselor can explore these next seven areas at any one point during the DRH or at different points along the time line.

Personality Issues

We are concerned about how each partner experiences the other's personality, and whether there are aspects that each tries to change in the other. Is jealousy a problem? Has one or the other seen the prospective partner become jealous over the other's behavior? What has been done about that?

A second area in which couples frequently struggle is anger. How does each see the other's temper? Who becomes the most angry? How does each know when the other is angry? Has one tried to change or alter the manner in which the other expresses anger? Has this succeeded?

Another personality dynamic that frequently causes conflict is moodiness. How does each see the other in regard to moodiness? Does one seem more moody than the other? What brings on the moods? Does one try to help the other's moods? Does it work?

Related to the issue of moodiness is negativity and a sense of being down. We wonder whether one is more negative or down than the other. Who tries to help whom? How do they attempt to counteract the negativity? Does it succeed?

Finally, we wonder about stubbornness or bossy behavior. How does each see the other in regard to stubbornness? Who is the most stubborn? Who can influence whom the most? Who generally wins when push comes to shove?

All of these issues have something to do with each person's relative satisfaction or dissatisfaction with the other's personality. All couples will make some attempt to change the prospective mate. But when a couple has major, ongoing differences that result in repeated conflict and attempts to change the partner, it may be a sign that one has some basic dislike for who the other is.

Communication

Couples have different levels of satisfaction and functionality in regard to communication. Most premarital and remarital couples feel that they are communicating well because they are very much involved with each other and very much interested in the other person. Nonetheless, some couples have more difficulty achieving good communication patterns than do others. During the course of the DRH, the counselor needs to assess the functionality of the communication pattern.

We are concerned about whether the partners believe they have open communication. Are they able to express their feelings? Can they say whatever is on their minds? Or do they find it difficult to express what they really feel? Does one shut the other off when communication reaches difficult or touchy areas?

Some people tend to be much more private and therefore inhibited when it comes to disclosing what they really think and feel. This pattern may not be pathological, but might instead be prevalent in the family of origin. Nonetheless, differences in regard to openness and closedness can create conflict. Is one more closed than the other? Is one more private and less open? Has this caused conflict? How has one tried to change this quality in the other? Has it succeeded?

Still another aspect of the communication pattern that we explore is the use of silence. Some families and some people use silence, particularly when they are angry, annoyed, or disappointed with the other. In some families, people may not speak for several days or even weeks. Thus, we are concerned as to whether the couple has experienced such silence. Who has become silent? How long did it last? How did they begin speaking again? Was the origin of the silence discovered? How did the recipient of the silent treatment feel? This is an important area because silence can be one of the most vicious forms of anger and can be received with a real sense of panic.

Lastly, we also like to explore the manner in which the couple handles criticism, either in terms of giving it or receiving it. Does either partner tend to attack the other? If so, who attacks whom? Or are they mutually attacking?

Conflict Resolution

Conflict is part of marital relationships, but premarital and remarital couples often have limited conflict. This is partly because when couples are in a state of bliss, commonly referred to as being "madly in love," they seek agreement and suppress disagreement, and partly because couples have fewer stresses at this point in their life, especially when they are young and marrying for the first time.

In any case, the premarital or remarital couple who has some experience in conflict resolution prior to the wedding is more likely to have a satisfactory adjustment to marriage because of their ability to resolve conflicts.

Therefore, we ask about the kinds of conflicts the couple has experienced. Many couples report few or no conflicts. For those who report that the relationship has been all positive with no conflict, we comment that conflict and argument are part of marriage. Two individuals cannot live in a relationship without disagreement and conflict. The issue is not whether the couple experiences conflict, but rather whether they have developed a method of resolving conflicts.

For those couples who have experienced conflict, we like to explore the following issues. Can each speak his or her mind to the other? Does one hold back? Why? If each can speak his or her mind, does the other understand? Can they each get their point across? And when it comes to resolving differences, how do they go about it? Does each give? Do they take turns giving in? Does one give in more than the other? Sometimes in relationships one person speaks his or her mind more than the other. When this happens, we wonder whether one is more concerned with avoiding conflict. Does one give in so as to avoid conflict? How did this get started? Does it work for them?

Financial Management

As in the area of conflict, some couples report few or no disagreements around issues of financial management. For some couples, this is an area in which they have very similar ideas and behaviors. Perhaps they come from similar families of origin. For other couples, conflict over financial management has not arisen because they have not had to make decisions and therefore have not been in situations in which conflict could arise. Still other couples have had disagreements over financial management.

We are concerned about how each partner deals with and reacts to how the other spends money. How does each see the other's spending habits? Does one spend too much or too little? How are the partners similar and different in this area? If they are different, how have they resolved the difference to date? What plans do they have to resolve the difference in the future?

Some couples have been living together prior to the wedding; inquire as to whether they split their expenses or merge their income. If they have merged their income, how have they resolved who did what in regard to financial management? Who banks the money? Who writes the checks? Who has how much spending money? Who has veto power over purchases? Do they like the manner in which they have handled the money? Has it worked out for them?

For couples who have kept their money separate, how do they intend to handle their money after the wedding? If they merge the money, who will write the checks? Who will bank the money? How will they make decisions about purchases?

To couples who have been involved in financial decision making of one kind or another during the premarital process, the area of financial management will have greater reality. To couples who are living with parents and not having to confront many decisions in the area of financial management, this particular topic may seem a bit abstract.

Leisure Activities

Each couple must find some way to deal with their similarities and differences regarding leisure time activities and hobbies. One area of potential conflict involves the degree with which the partners need to share hobbies or activities, or whether they can each do their own separately.

We therefore explore the degree of similarity or difference in their hobbies and interests. Does one pressure the other to enjoy certain activities? Do they feel they do too much together? Or do they feel they do too much separately? Can they find a balance? Have they attempted to do so? Sometimes partners feel that mates are either too busy or too inactive. Has there been struggle in this area? Does one feel the other has too many activities? Does one feel the other has too few activities? Sometimes couples have a different sense of what "having fun" means and will therefore disagree over having a good time. Is the couple similar or different in this area? Have they had any struggles over the nature of having a good time?

Some couples have many leisure activities, but feel cheated when it comes to enjoying each other. Other couples spend a lot of time with each other but feel they are not active enough in terms of hobbies and activities. In other words, each couple must find some way to balance togetherness and separateness. How has this couple experienced this issue? Do they spend enough time together? Does one feel left out? Do they ever feel that they have had too much time alone?

For some couples, this discussion will be only theoretical. Because premarital and remarital couples usually can't get enough time together, they have no desire to spend time alone. Couples who have lived together prior to the wedding can discuss this area with a greater sense of reality because they have already had to struggle with balancing togetherness and separateness. In any case, each marital couple has to decide for themselves how much togetherness they need, and when they need it.

Sexual and Affectional Relationship

With more couples marrying later, the percentage of couples cohabiting before the wedding increases. In addition, more couples are also sexually active prior to the wedding. Prewedding sexual behavior may pose a philosophical problem for clergy. In the premarital and remarital counseling context, however, the issue should not be whether sexual activity is appropriate but rather how functional this area of the relationship is.

In addition to discussing the sexual relationship, it is also very necessary to address and differentiate the affectional aspect of the relationship. Has the couple been satisfied with the amount of affection expressed during the relationship? Has either of them felt unloved? How have they attempted to go about getting more love? Has it worked?

As we move along the time line, we simply ask couples if and when they started having sexual intercourse. If they are not yet sexually active, how have they managed that? Do they feel that they are meeting their affectional and sexual needs as a "team" or couple, or is this an area of power struggles? Once the couple has indicated that they have been sexually active, then we inquire about whether the amount of sexual activity is satisfactory. If not, why not? Has the amount of sexual activity changed as they have moved toward the wedding?

When the couple became sexually active, was each comfortable with the sexual activity? Was either uncomfortable? Did each know about the other's discomfort? We ask the couple whether they discussed becoming sexually active before first having sex. If so, what did they decide? If they did not talk about it before they first had sex, why? Did they discuss it afterward? Have they been able to talk about their sexual relationship at all? Would they characterize their conversations about sex as open or difficult and tense?

Ideally, couples who have been sexually active will also have talked about birth control. Some sexually active couples, however, will not have discussed this area. We think it important to explore the couple's level of communication about contraception. Have they used a birth control method? If so, which one? How did they arrive at that choice? Have they discussed other options? Are they satisfied with any methods they have employed? Would they like to make changes? Has there been an unplanned pregnancy? Was there a miscarriage, abortion, or adoption? How do they see this impacting their relationship now?

Birth control and family planning are also topics to be raised with the premarital couple who is not yet sexually active. Have they discussed birth control and the best times to conceive or avoid pregnancy? The counselor can reword some of the above questions as appropriate for these couples to help them explore this topic.

Family and Friends

Each couple has to find some way to deal with the separate circle of friends that each partner may have before becoming involved with the other. Some couples find it difficult to merge their friendship circles because one does not like the other's friends. We think it important to check out how the couple has merged their friendship network. We wonder whether each likes the other's friends. Has each felt pressured to like the other's friends?

In addition to finding a way of dealing with the other's friendship network, each partner must decide whether there are friends with whom they can socialize individually or whether they must socialize with all friends as a couple. Thus, we wonder whether they have allowed each other to socialize individually with some friends. Must they always socialize as a couple? If they can socialize individually, have any friends taken up too much time? Have they fought over whether one is spending more time with friends than with the other partner?

Each couple must also balance the amount of time spent with families of origin as opposed to time spent with each other. Although we will explore families of origin further in Chapter Five, at this point in the DRH we are interested in how they have experienced the involvement with the families of origin. Does each feel the other is too involved with his or her parents? Does each feel the other is too influenced by what his or her parents say? Is each comfortable with his or her prospective in-laws? Have the partners found a way to resolve any differences in these areas?

Interactional Patterns

We have been outlining some areas of focus that the premarital and remarital counselor should examine as he or she proceeds along the time line, exploring the history of the relationship. Although we have occasionally made comments as to why we ask the questions we do, we now want to address what the counselor should watch for as the relationship unfolds before his or her eyes.

Bonding

In Chapter Two, we discussed bonding. Here we want to point out that while conducting the DRH, we are interested in observing how the bonding process took place and whether it has followed a usual or common pattern, or has the marks of being abnormal or difficult. As we indicated earlier, if the bonding process follows a rather typical development, the three stages of commitment will be evident during the dating history. The counselor can easily spot difficulties in moving through the three stages. When a couple has difficulty moving from one stage to another, they may separate. The partners may develop other relationships, which can intervene in or prevent the movement to another stage. It is important for the counselor to characterize difficulties in the couple's bonding process during the wrap-up.

Sometimes counselors use *bonding* and *commitment* interchangeably, but they are different. Bonding is the chemistry that causes a couple to be drawn together. That is why we have referred to it as glue. Commitment follows bonding and is more rational because it is intentional.

Dependency

Another factor that we bear in mind when watching a couple lay out their relationship has to do with the dependency needs of these two people. How dependent are they on each other? Are they able to articulate their dependency needs? Do they make them clear? Part of the answers to these questions lies in observing the speed of the dating relationship.

Couples who are relatively independent people, who want a relationship but do not need it, follow a deliberate course as they proceed through the premarital process. Couples with exaggerated dependency needs often take one of two courses. For some, the dependency needs are so strong that they no longer just want but desperately need the other person, and rush to the third stage of commitment. For others, the dependency needs are so profound that they postpone the commitment process, fearful of being swallowed up in the relationship. They exaggerate the length of the courtship to protect their own esteem.

We have often found that it helps couples if we raise questions about their dependency needs. We often ask them to comment on how they see each other's needs, which seems more informative than asking each to talk about his or her own dependency needs. We sometimes ask John how he sees Mary: How would he rate her on a scale from one to ten in terms of her dependency needs? And the same for Mary: How does she see John? How would she rate him on a scale from one to ten? Self-awareness about dependency needs is a goal of the DRH and the counselor can comment on this aspect in the wrap-up session.

Self-Esteem and Communication

Another issue that we think the counselor should keep in mind is self-esteem. Whether each partner sees himself or herself as a person of worth will influence the communication process. The decision-making processes that couples go through reflect each partner's level of self-esteem. Individuals with good self-esteem speak up; they want mutual decisions about what the couple does and where they go. Individuals with low self-esteem frequently take one of two courses. On the one hand, they often hesitate to speak up with their opinion, because they do not want to be thought stupid or crazy or they do not want to irritate and alienate the prospective mate.

Relationships in which one or both partners have low self-esteem are frequently marked by an absence of conflict in the decision-making process, or by the partners' difficulty in making decisions because neither will speak up. On the other hand, some individuals with low self-esteem compensate for this by being determined to have their own way. They cover their weakness with a kind of dominance. This person can be spotted in a couple in which either one person makes all the decisions or both chronically argue about their plans. We have often found it helpful to ask each person to comment on how they perceive the other's self-esteem.

Power

The decision-making process is affected not only by each person's self-esteem but also by the whole issue of power. During the dating process, couples frequently like to think that neither is going to have more power than the other, that they are going to have a fifty-fifty relationship. However, whenever two people are intimately involved, the issues of power, leadership, and control lie beneath the surface.

As we watch the dating relationship unfold, we observe the nature of power in the relationship. The decision-making process is one area in which the issue of power is most clearly visible. As the couple decides how often they will date, where they will go, what they will do, and then, later in the relationship, what they will buy and when they will buy it, their way of making these choices will reflect issues of power. We find it helpful to raise some questions about that with couples. We try to determine who is in charge of the relationship now, how each of them sees the other in regard to power, and whether the couple, too, wonders who is in charge.

Intimacy

Another factor that demonstrates itself clearly in a DRH is the dynamic of intimacy. Intimacy functions in several areas, for example, physical, emotional, cognitive, and spiritual areas. Has the couple been able to establish an intimate relationship, a closeness, a togetherness, that is healthy?

When couples have difficulty with intimacy, it manifests in two common ways. Some couples become too close—they absorb each other. These people become obsessed with each other, knowing intuitively each other's thoughts and feelings. To some extent, this is normal for premarital couples. Nonetheless, some couples clearly are too absorbed in each other. One can predict that at some point in the future, one or both will feel smothered unless they develop more room for individuality in their relationship. Such a couple can benefit from questions designed to raise their awareness about their intense closeness. Can they function when the other is gone for a few days? How much time alone do they each need every day? Can they engage in separate activities and not feel lonely?

On the other hand, some couples have difficulty becoming close or intimate. These couples set up barriers or distancing behaviors designed to keep them from becoming too close. Anger, arguments, infrequent contact, separations, and continued dating of other people are some behaviors couples use to keep distant.

We have found it helpful to raise questions about closeness. We try to determine how a couple experiences their intimacy, whether they each feel smothered, or whether they feel too distant and lonely. Sometimes we ask each person to rate on a scale from one to ten the level of intimacy at different points in their common history.

Religious Practice

In the course of a dating relationship, many issues arise that can produce arguments because of the couple's potential for differences of opinion. Areas such as the handling of money, the use of alcohol and other chemical substances, and the disciplining of children are often possible battlegrounds. One such area is the issue of religion and religious practice.

Clergy who serve as premarital and remarital counselors may want to focus on religion and religious practice at some point during the DRH. In order to help each person become aware of the other's perspective, it is important to establish a dual focus: religion and religious practice. Couples may share similar religious thoughts or theological frameworks, but differ widely in practice. On the other hand, couples can have similar religious practices, but very different philosophical or theological values.

We have found it helpful for couples to explore their religious value systems. Sometimes we have each try to articulate what the other believes or values. It will quickly become apparent to the couple how much each knows about the other's thoughts or values. The discussion will naturally flow, then, into each partner's description of his or her own religious thoughts and beliefs. The clergy member can pose specific questions about denominational beliefs. If the partners are of the same religious background, the pastor's questions can help them see how each agrees or differs with the religious background. If they are from different religious backgrounds, the clergy member's questions can help them assess their similarities and differences in doctrinal beliefs.

The process of helping the couple to examine their similarities and differences in regard to religion and religious values is to be repeated in the area of religious practice. Again, the clergy member should explore the areas of agreement or disagreement. What were the partners' religious practices or activities in high school? After high school? Was each a member of a church, synagogue, or religious group? How frequently did he or she attend— never, once a month, or twice a year? What about future plans? Will both attend the same church or religious group after marriage? How often? What about religious commitment as measured by willingness to donate time to teach Sunday school or to pay tithes or offerings?

We suggest that at this point in the DRH, clergy restrict their work simply to helping the couple explore their similarities and differences in religious values and practices. This topic is also addressed in PREPARE and FOCCUS and can be examined in Part 5 of our model—the wedding preparation.

The Wrap-Up Session

When we have completed a DRH, we spend some time sharing our observations with the couple. The wrap-up is not to be judgmental or critical but descriptive. We have found that couples benefit enormously from hearing an outsider or third party comment on their relationship. This kind of information is often helpful for couples, giving them some new sense about themselves and their relationship.

Counselors who use inventories or assessment devices should incorporate the information from the instrument or instruments into the wrap-up. Such information will bring another point of view into the summarization, which will likely make the information seem more complete and objective. Counselors using PREPARE, PREPARE-MC, or MATE will have a wealth of information from the inventory that is parallel to what we are assessing in the DRH. We recommend that those counselors use the inventory results and information while doing the DRH and throughout the counseling sessions. For counselors who might follow the counseling outline suggested in the PREPARE, PREPARE-MC, or MATE *Counselor Feedback Guide,* we suggest that they use the dyadic questioning techniques to enhance their feedback sessions with couples.

Developing a wrap-up of a relationship requires the counselor to blend his or her creative and artistic talents with deductive and scientific ones. The counselor may want to use succinct analogies and metaphors. The most important element in the wrap-up is presenting the couple with an analysis of their relationship that is different from and more comprehensive than their own analysis.

The wrap-up must be bilateral. The best wrap-ups include all of the major aspects of the couple's interactional system and include how both partners were involved in creating the couple's system. That involvement may be active or passive, but nonetheless, both partners carved out their couple system.

Be sure to use examples from the DRH to support your view of the couple's relationship. Use individual and couple strengths from the DRH. The DRH produces much data. Use it. If you are, for example, concerned about a couple's pattern of distancing each other, cite the many separations they have had and may continue to have. For example, a couple in a small town planned to live in an apartment above the man's parents' business. The husband-to-be was already at his father's beck and call. Even though he was twenty-eight years old, it was as if he were eighteen. He was more involved with his dad and the family business than with his fiancée. The counselor used this observation in the wrap-up, which had profound, growth-inducing results for the couple.

Be sure that you develop a wrap-up that is at the couple's level of seeing the world. Use metaphors with couples who are not very cognitive, for example, and who would not benefit from a cognitive or highly intellectualized analysis of their relationship.

It is also important to match the theme of the wrap-up to the couple. The wrap-up, in some general way, has to "fit" the couple. If the wrap-up and accompanying reframe are too far off-base, they will fall flat with the couple.

It is difficult to make the written word reflect the kind of life and excitement that the DRH can have in reality. This process is both easy and fun to use. As a rule of thumb, we feel that if the counselor is enjoying himself or herself, the couple is probably learning from the experience.

We have said that the purpose of premarital and remarital counseling is not to resolve all conflict or issues. Rather, the purpose is to make the couple aware of issues and patterns, giving them a new way to understand them and some skills to deal with them. We hope we have underscored the issue of awareness as we have unfolded the DRH. It raises questions the couple has not raised, opens up areas the couple has not discussed, and expands their thinking about the nature of their relationship. If the counselor can accomplish these tasks, the couple will walk into the future armed with better skills for dealing with their relationship.

In this chapter we have introduced the procedure for premarital and remarital counseling. We have presented in detail the methodology for doing the Dynamic Relationship History, which is a structured way of looking at a relationship's history from the time the couple first met up to the present. The purpose of the DRH is to help the couple become aware of how they behave with each other and affect each other, and what interactional patterns they have developed. The DRH also provides the counselor with useful information for the counseling process. In the next chapter we continue to develop and outline our model and methodology for premarital and remarital counseling.

Chapter Five

Exploring the Family of Origin and Previous Relationships

In this chapter we cover Part 3 of the premarital and remarital counseling process—the family-of-origin exploration (FOE). We then detail the other parts of the counseling process. Before we move into the process of the family-of-origin work, we briefly note the theoretical issues behind this particular aspect.

Separation from Family of Origin

It has been well established in family theory and family therapy theory that the degree of separation a person has from his or her family of origin can be an important indicator of marital success. The degree to which a person can move in status from child to adult, to become a peer with his or her parents, has something to do with that individual's ability to succeed in marriage.

Earlier Cultures

In preindustrial societies, the degree of closeness to one's family of origin influenced the success of one's marriage. In such societies, the family existed as an extended unit, with more than one generation in a household. Thus, the family functioned more as a clan. The clan was the depository of knowledge. If young people were to survive the rigors of life, they depended on the clan to teach them the necessary survival skills and to provide the appropriate support for that survival. It was difficult for individuals or a couple to survive outside of a clan. In preindustrial societies, therefore, the individual's connection with and incorporation into the clan were extremely important. In psychological terms, enmeshment in the clan was not only necessary but positive.

Preindustrial societies also did not experience change as it is experienced today. Life was more static; change came about more slowly. The oldest generations of the family could function as appropriate transmitters of knowledge and survival skills. The knowledge passed on by the oldest generation might be valid for centuries.

Twentieth-Century Cultures

The industrial revolution, which began in the eighteenth century, dramatically affected not only society, but family life as well. The advent of the steam engine brought the development of the machine. The machine brought the factory. The factory brought the movement from farm to town. With the nineteenth and twentieth centuries, increasing industrialization and technological advances made mobility and change a part of life.

In preindustrial cultures, the family was relatively immobile. People were born, were reared, got married, and lived and died in the same home. With the industrial society and the mobility that resulted from it, the clan was disrupted. The enmeshment that was positive in a preindustrial society becomes a liability in an industrial society. Too much enmeshment prevents individuals and couples from appropriate involvement in an industrial society, which demands that people move and change.

It is no longer innovative to talk about the rapid change that is part of our lifestyle. We are familiar with and must continually deal with a quickly changing world. Our changing world means a change in knowledge. Because of this, parents no longer have wisdom that remains fixed and unchanging for centuries. Slowly but surely, experts in a variety of fields have taken the place of the family as the depository of knowledge. Parents' ways of doing things may no longer be best, adequate, or right for children.

The industrial revolution and mobility have made the clan obsolete. It is no longer necessary for survival. A properly trained individual in an industrial society no longer needs the large support group of the clan either to succeed or to survive in life. In the preindustrial age, the clan was of paramount importance, and individuals were of secondary importance. In an industrial society, the individual has much more importance, as does marriage.

An industrialized society, therefore, requires a new kind of maturity on the part of individuals. With the clan no longer around either to provide support or to help with survival, both physical and emotional survival depend on the responsibility and maturity of the individual.

Research and Clinical Impact

Since the early 1950s, significant research and clinical observation has been done in family theory and therapy on the importance of individuals' ability to separate psychologically from their families of origin. Many couple and family therapists have incorporated these family-of-origin concepts into their clinical work.[1]

The people who adapt to marital life best in America seem to have two characteristics. First, they have been able to leave home, psychologically speaking. By "leaving home," we mean that the individuals no longer ask their parents to take responsibility for their lives. To put it in other terms, these individuals have become adults and no longer ask their parents to mother and father them. Second, people who best adapt to American marital life have had an opportunity to live alone after they have left home and before they enter marriage. Living alone and being able to survive both emotionally and financially are important in that people must have an opportunity to establish their own psychological identity.

Individuals who have not left home emotionally and psychologically will experience greater difficulties in life in a number of ways. First, they keep getting tangled up in family problems. Their own marital relationships are chronically in crisis because of crises in the larger family. Struggles between mother and father, between parents and one or more of the children, or between adult children interfere with and cause friction in the marriage.

Second, people who have not left home psychologically tend to look for spouses who will continue parenting them. Because families that hang onto their children prevent their children from growing up psychologically, these individuals look for a spouse not in terms of a peer, a fellow adult with whom they can establish an intimate relationship, but in terms of someone who will take care of them. That kind of relationship is frequently beset with problems, because chances are that the other spouse is looking for the very same kind of partner. Thus, two people who are both looking for a parent depend on each other to be the good, kind, and patient parent who will enable them to be a child forever.

Third, people who have not left home psychologically tend to have more physical and somatic problems than others. The research on psychosomatic illness documents that people who are still emotionally entangled with their families of origin as adults are sick more frequently than those who are more independent.

Fourth, people who have not psychologically separated from their parents usually come from homes in which the parents do not want them to do so. They have been encouraged not to grow up, not to take charge of their own lives, to remain children. With this attitude in the family of origin, the young adult will have difficulty functioning as an adult.

Part 3: Family-of-Origin Exploration

The purpose of Part 3 of our premarital and remarital counseling process is to look at the degree of separation that exists between each of the persons and their family of origin. Part 3 is designed to help the couple assess whether they come from a clan, whether they have an excessive attachment to their parents, and whether they will be able to take responsibility for their own lives. It should also give them some sense of their need for growth regarding their family of origin.

Parents' Model for Marriage

Parents are the first human beings that we, as children, come to know. Father is the first male and Mother is the first female we come to know. Our parents are also the first husband-wife team we know. From Father, we observe what husbanding is all about. From Mother, we observe what wifing is all about.

Marital expectations, marital attitudes, and marital behavior patterns are not innately instilled in us. We learn them from parents. Children who have only one parent, or whose parents are absent or deficient in some way, creatively find substitutes or significant others such as grandparents, aunts, uncles, neighbors, and teachers.

The research on family theory and therapy clearly indicates that parents are powerful models. Naturally, some models are better than others. Thus, parents in an indirect fashion either help or hinder couples in establishing and maintaining married life.

When conflict exists in the parental marriage, the children tend to take one of two courses. On the one hand, some of the children will repeat the pattern of the parental marriage. It is almost as if children who see their parents struggling with problems they cannot resolve need to duplicate those problems or patterns and attempt to solve them for themselves and for their parents. On the other hand, some people try to avoid the conflicts of their parents' marriage by behaving in exactly the opposite ways. Sometimes that works, and at other times it only creates the opposite problems.

If, as people grow up, they perceive their same-sex parent as losing in the marital relationship, they seem to experience a particular kind of pain. Although marriages are usually well balanced, and husband and wife either both lose or both win, children often do not perceive it that way. If the same-sex parent was perceived as losing, the adult child may be difficult to live with because he or she does not want to duplicate the losing. In like manner, the adult child who saw the same-sex parent winning may seek to dominate or get his or her own way.

In the family-of-origin exploration, our purpose is not only to look at and trace the parental models that a man and woman bring into their relationship, but also to trace how these models influence their behavior with each other. We seek to heighten the couple's awareness of the models.

Administrative Issues and the FOE

In our outline of the premarital and remarital counseling process, we place the FOE after the DRH. The reader may be wondering why the family-of-origin work does not come first. We have placed it second because frequently the counselor does not know one or both parties. The DRH acquaints the counselor with the couple.

People seem to find it easier and they appear to be more motivated to talk about themselves and their dating experience than about their family of origin. Since most couples have experienced their dating relationship as pleasant and are in a state of heightened awareness about their relationship as they move toward the wedding, this is often an easier starting place for them.

There are some families in which the parental closeness and attachment to the young adult children is so intense that the children will resist any attempt to discuss the family. The young adults often feel that they should not talk about the parents without their explicit approval. The adult children may also feel that what happens in the family of origin is no one else's business.

It is important for the premarital and remarital counselor to explain the reasons for the FOE as clearly and as fully as possible. The counselor should stress the impact of parental modeling. Most individuals will, upon reflection, see the usefulness of the FOE. Others will remain resistant. If a person or couple is resistant, it is best to respect their feelings and not push the FOE. Often, focusing on the reason for these feelings will overcome the resistance. If necessary, the counselor can also conduct the FOE alone with the willing partner and can focus on both families. When only one partner is present, it is important, however, for the counselor also to focus on what the reluctant partner's behavior might mean for the future marriage. Such predictions will help the person reflect on the implications of the partner's behavior.

In terms of the basic format for the FOE, we suggest devoting almost two sessions to the FOE process. One session can be devoted to each family. We also suggest, as an optional unit, adding one counseling session in which the parents can say good-bye to their single child and hello to the married couple.

Looking at each person's family of origin means examining all the interactions and all the levels of functioning in the family. In most premarital and remarital counseling cases, this will not be difficult to accomplish, unless the family has many children, or unless many marriages, divorces, and other events make the family of origin harder to comprehend.

We divide the family-of-origin exploration into seven sections: (1) siblings as individuals, (2) sibling interactions, (3) parent-child interactions, (4) husband-wife interactions, (5) family interactional styles, (6) parental models, and (7) the wrap-up.

Method of the FOE

As in the DRH, we have found that visual aids are important in effectively dealing with this material. We suggest using either a blackboard or newsprint. Since the counselor will want to keep the diagram for future reference, using paper will save the task of copying the information from the blackboard.

At the beginning of the FOE, the counselor draws the family as a two-generation genogram. Our basic format is shown in Figures 5.1 and 5.2, which illustrate John and Mary's separate families. From Figure 5.1, the reader can see that John is twenty-one years old and has two older brothers—Joe who is twenty-three, and Mike who is twenty-six and married to Ellen. John has one younger sister, Susan, who is eighteen. John's parents are Henry, forty-eight, and Elsie, forty-six. Similar information is given for Mary and her family in Figure 5.2.

There has been much interest in using genograms in marriage and family therapy. As a result, the format has become standardized.[2] As we use the genogram in our premarital and remarital FOE, we use both the two-generational figure-type diagrams shown in Figures 5.1 and 5.2, and the standardized format shown in Figure 5.3. We have found that we can greatly personalize the FOE process by adding faces or similar attributes to the figure-type diagramming when discussing and drawing the couple and their families of origin. Thought, creativity, and humor seem to flow when we use the personalized figures in comparison to the square and circle format. We do use the standardized square and circle symbols as we expand the chart to include the details of three or four generations.

Using the symbols and notations that have become standardized in genograms, Figure 5.3 shows John and Mary in their families of origin. The information shows the engaged couple, John and Mary, and family information as far back as their grandparents. The reader can easily determine that both John and Mary come from intact families, the only divorce having been Mary's

Figure 5.1. John in His Family of Origin.

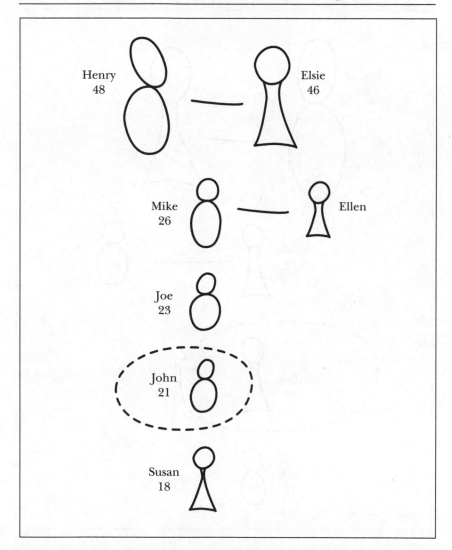

Aunt Agnes. John's family of origin, with four children, is the largest for either family line in the three generations shown. Apparently, the families are healthy in that only Mary's Grandpa Bart and one other person are deceased. The genogram shows that Grandpa Bart died of cancer in 1984 at the age of 69. One of Mary's cousins, the middle child of Uncle Judd and Aunt Judy, is dead, but Mary could not recall the reason for the death.

Figure 5.2. Mary in Her Family of Origin.

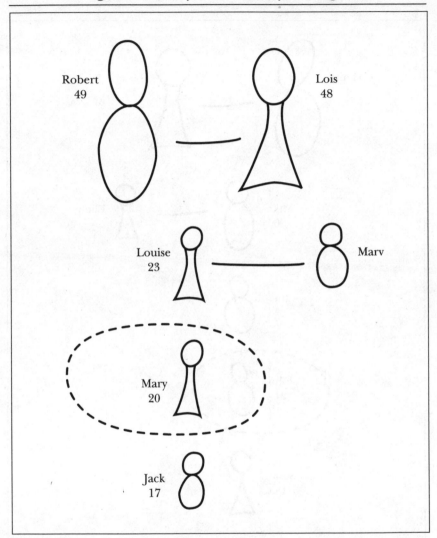

The genogram also shows the birth order position of each family member and the gender of siblings. John is the third child and third son of four children. Mary is the second child and second daughter of three children. What might be the implications for their relationship? Both are middle children and thus have had experience interacting with others. Yet both have same-gender older siblings and an opposite-gender younger sibling. Perhaps John and

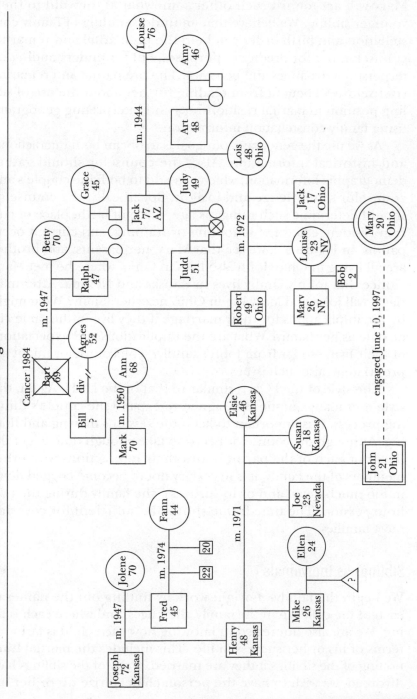

Figure 5.3. Standard Genogram Showing John and Mary and Their Families of Origin for Three Generations.

Mary will act toward each other somewhat as they did to their younger sibling. We believe that an understanding of family constellation and birth order can help the premarital and remarital counselor, not for predictive purposes, but for understanding interpersonal dynamics and behavior. The premarital and remarital counselor will benefit from reading further about the use of sibling position in marital relationships and interpreting genograms using family constellation information.[3]

As we use the genogram, our goal is to obtain both interactional and historical information. Also, the counselor should gather demographic information, which can add to both the couple's and counselor's knowledge and insight. Specifically, the counselor should determine such things as age, place of birth, place of current residence, level of schooling or training, and current occupation. In Figure 5.3, we see that Mary, her parents, and brother are all living in Ohio. John also lives in Ohio, where he met Mary. Notice that John's family lives in Kansas and Nevada. After marriage, will John and Mary live in Ohio near her family? What might be the implications for their marriage if they live in the same city or state as her family? What are the implications and expectations of their living so far from John's family? The counselor might appropriately raise such issues.

The style of the FOE is similar to that of the DRH. Again, this style uses many questions designed to expand the couple's thinking process. It is important to keep the sessions moving and flowing. Although the counselor needs to take enough time to get the flavor of each of the partners and their interactions with other members of the family, it is necessary not to become bogged down in too much detail and or to "process" the family during the two-hour session. The time frame should be sufficient for covering most families.

Siblings as Individuals

We begin the family-of-origin work by finding out the names of each of the children in the family, their ages, and where each is living. We are also interested in knowing how each child is faring in terms of his or her success in life. This includes the marital functioning of the siblings if they are married. If any of the siblings have divorced, we wish to have the person characterize his or her understanding of the marital conflict and subsequent divorce. We also want each person to characterize the personality and temperament of his or her siblings. Are they outgoing or shy, talkative or quiet, easily angered or even-tempered, assertive or passive, opinionated or agreeable?

The issue in this particular segment is how separated siblings are from the family of origin. Generally speaking, the children who function the best in adulthood and succeed in marital life are those who have been able to separate somewhat from the family of origin. Sometimes we can ascertain that by geography. The children who are within shouting distance of parents or who have gone to the farthest part of the earth are often those who have had the most difficulty with parents and leaving home. The counselor should get some idea of the degree to which other family members have been able to leave home psychologically.

Sibling Interactions

In this particular segment, we are primarily interested in how the children in the family got along with each other during childhood. Our process is to take the oldest child and look at his or her relationship to the second oldest child, the third oldest child, and so on. Then we take the second oldest child and look at his or her relationship to the oldest child, the third oldest child, the fourth oldest child, and on down. We use all the combinations of each child and his or her relationship to every other child until the entire sibling system is explored.

The issue in our study of these dyads has to do with the manner in which these individuals related to each other while growing up and whether or not any of the children in the family functioned in a substitute-parent role. If a person has developed a close, primary relationship with an older child, separating from that sibling can pose as many problems as leaving the relationship with parents. It is also possible that the child who has functioned as a substitute parent will have difficulty moving into a relationship in which he or she cannot continue to function in a caretaking role.

We are also concerned about the spacing of the children. If more than five years separate children, it is likely that one or both might have experienced life in an isolated way, as an only child does. On the other hand, if children are closely spaced and if there are many of them, they may have felt deprived of attention.

Parent-Child Interactions

The purpose of this section is to examine the past relationship between each parent and each child in the family. We want to get an idea of how the parent and child interacted. How did they get along? How did they express anger toward each other? How did they express affection toward each other? Who won when they fought? How were they similar or dissimilar from each other?

In addition to exploring the kind of interaction each parent had with each child, we are particularly interested in each person's perception of the parents' preference order for their children. In other words, we are interested in knowing from John whom he thinks his father liked best and why, and whom his mother liked best and why. If the partner has been around the family enough to comment on this issue, we ask for that partner's perception of whom John's mother liked best, whom his father liked best, and vice versa. It is valuable to ask about whom each parent liked least and why. Again, double-check the perception with the partner's opinion.

The issue here is the role of favor in the family. People who are the parent's first choice—the favorites—often have stronger attachments to the parent. Sometimes parents attach their ambitions and dreams to the favorite child and try to live vicariously through him or her. Favorite children may find it more difficult to leave home or to have the parent allow them to leave home.

One should not overlook, however, the role of negative attachment. It is also possible that in the dislike for a parent, a child can maintain a negative attachment to him or her, even though positive attachments are denied. The child who feels that he or she is never good enough has a kind of attachment to parents, just as the child who never does wrong has a strong bond. Again, the issue of attachment has something to do with the psychological freedom of the child in adulthood.

Husband-Wife Interactions

In this section, we are particularly interested in the nature of the parents' marital relationship. Our interest in this is very similar to our interest in the relationship of the premarital couple. We wonder about power: Who was in charge of the marriage? How did they handle decision making? How was the power balanced? What about anger? How did the child know when Mother was angry with Father, or when Father was angry with Mother? What happened when they argued? Who got hurt? Who made up? Who initiated peace overtures? Or, if the husband and wife did not argue, how did they demonstrate their disagreement? Where did it come out? How far underground was it? How about affection? How did each child know when Father was pleased with what Mother said and did, or when Mother was pleased with what Father said and did? How comfortable were the parents with affection? Could they both give it and receive it? How about self-esteem? How did each person perceive the level of self-esteem in Father? In Mother? If low self-esteem was present, how did this affect the relationship? Was each parent oversensitive? Was each vulnerable? How, then, did they handle their pain? How parents handled anger, affection, self-esteem, dependency, closeness, and many other issues will have an impact on adult children. Parents will have provided a model; in many subtle ways, the model will have affected the children.

The quality of the parents' marriage has quite an influence on the children. If the marital relationship is or was good and the coalition between Mother and Father has been firm and healthy, the parents will be able to let their children grow up and establish their own lives. If, however, the marital relationship is not good, if it has turned bitter or sour, then one or both parents will frequently attempt to attach themselves to one of the children to make up for what is not happening in the marriage. If there is a psychological split in the parents' marital relationship, whether or not it leads to a divorce, there is a high possibility that one or more of the children will be chosen as a surrogate or substitute spouse.

Children who are chosen to fill the role of a spouse because of a bad marriage have difficulty leaving home. Psychologically, the parents in a crippled marriage will attempt to rescue some sense of hope, happiness, and esteem from a child. If a parent has attempted to make a child a substitute mate, it is a kind of psychological marriage. The child will have difficulty moving to his or her own marriage unless he or she can divorce from the marriage with the parent. It is difficult enough being married to one spouse, let alone two.

Family Interactional Styles

In this section, we are interested in two dynamics of the family of origin: flexibility and closeness (connectedness). These two relationship dimensions are presented graphically in Figure 5.4. This figure shows the scored results for a sample couple who have taken the PREPARE inventory. The plotting of the couple's scores shows how both partners perceive their own family of origin as well as their current relationship together.

As Figure 5.4 shows, in taking the PREPARE inventory, the female partner describes her family of origin (F-FO) as "somewhat flexible" and "overly connected." The male describes his family of origin (M-FO) as "very flexible" and "disconnected." Here the counselor would have information that this couple has come from very different families, particularly along the closeness dimension. What are the implications of this for the couple's relationship? This is good information to use in continuing the FOE portion of counseling.

Also, when this couple took PREPARE, they described their current relationship on the same two dimensions. Figure 5.4 reflects that the female partner describes their relationship (F-CR) as "somewhat flexible" and "very connected," while the male describes the relationship (M-CR) as "flexible" and "connected." Here, the couple is describing the relationship quite similarly in that their scores are in adjoining categories. In the counseling situation, the counselor would have a sense of the accuracy of these scores from having done the DRH with the couple.

Flexibility

One goal of the FOE is to assess the flexibility of the family of origin. We focus on two aspects of that dynamic: leadership and rules. We explore whether leadership was missing and ambiguous, shared, or authoritarian. Was it easy to identify the leader or leaders in the family? Did the same person or persons exercise leadership roles during the childrearing years? Or did different individuals act as leaders at that time? Or was leadership equal? In some families, the leadership is ambiguous. Was it difficult to tell who was in charge of the family?

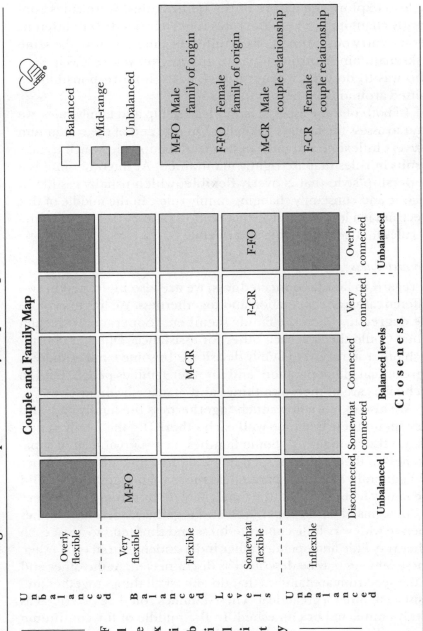

Figure 5.4. Couple and Family Map Example for the PREPARE Inventory.

Couple and Family Map

□ Balanced

▨ Mid-range

▓ Unbalanced

M-FO Male family of origin

F-FO Female family of origin

M-CR Male couple relationship

F-CR Female couple relationship

Flexibility

Unbalanced
Overly flexible

Balanced Levels
Very flexible
Flexible
Somewhat flexible

Unbalanced
Inflexible

Closeness

Unbalanced — Disconnected

Balanced levels — Somewhat connected | Connected | Very connected

Unbalanced — Overly connected

Note: From *Sample Counselor Report: Couple and Family Map*, 1996, Minneapolis, MN: Life Innovations. Reprinted by permission. Developed by David Olson at the University of Minnesota.

Leadership roles are connected with family rules and whether families maintain their rules rigidly or have no rules at all. Thus, we also explore the nature of the family rules. Were rules constantly changing, or were the rules relatively fixed? Did different people carry out various tasks at different times, or were the same tasks maintained throughout the growing-up years? Was it clear who was to do what when, or were household responsibilities shifted around from person to person?

In both of these aspects, family leadership and family rules, we want to assess the family's flexibility. On one end of the continuum is a very inflexible and unchanging leadership style, which usually results in rules that are rigidly maintained. At the other end is a leadership style that is overly flexible, which usually results in chaotic and constantly changing family rules. In the middle of this spectrum is a leadership style that is appropriately flexible and family rules that are also stable and flexible.

Connectedness

In regard to family connectedness, we are also interested in two different aspects: cooperation and togetherness. We like to explore the degree to which the family members cooperated with each other. Could they ask each other for assistance? Did they consult each other in regard to family decisions? In some families there is a great deal of cooperation, and in other families people tend to each take care of their own things and manage by themselves.

We also explore how much togetherness the family had. Did they spend their free time with each other? Did the family generally do things together? Some families have a great deal of separateness in their activities, spending little free time with each other and generally valuing separateness more than togetherness. Did the family feel close? Did the family feel distant from each other?

In terms of both cooperation and togetherness, some families operate with very little connectedness and thus tend to assist each other very little and operate rather independently from each other. These families may be described as disconnected. At the other end of the spectrum are families that do almost all things together and assist each other a great deal. These families could be described as overly connected or enmeshed. In the middle of the continuum are families that can operate both with some togetherness and some separateness, having a style that combines both independence and dependence and that we call connected.

Parental Models

At this point in the FOE, the premarital and remarital counselor should have a good sense of what kind of modeling the parents provided in psychological and interactional terms. Parents, however, are also models in such things as the demonstration of affection, the style of socializing, the use of alcohol and other chemical substances, the manner of disciplining children, the management of finances, and the practice of religion.

Clergy, in particular, may wish at this point in the counseling process to explore the models parents provided in religion and religious practice. However, the exploration of this area need not be limited to clergy, because it is an important area for all couples to explore. Again, the issue is twofold; what values or beliefs did parents directly or indirectly teach, and what were the religious practices of the home? Did both parents attend church? How often? What devotional behavior was part of the family pattern? Did the family pray before meals? These and many other questions can be asked to help the couple become more aware of the similarities and differences between the two families of origin and their expectations of each other about religion and religious practice.

Wrap-Up of the FOE

We have been attempting to outline a process for conducting the FOE. It is an orderly process, and one that is designed to establish how a family works and what makes it tick. We have attempted to show the reader some of the things we look for in our understanding of how families work. Although not all of this information is necessarily meant to be passed along to the couple, it will help the counselor understand the family life.

Each premarital or remarital counselor will probably see the same family in a somewhat different way. Each must respond to what he or she sees, what impresses him or her, what touches or concerns him or her. A counselor is interested in providing the young person with a new, different, and meaningful way of looking at and understanding his or her family. With this new perspective, the person can become more aware of the dynamics in the family of origin. This will help both partners expand their thinking about the nature of human relationships and their own relationship.

We have attempted to provide the premarital and remarital counselor with some theoretical background. We want to underscore again that one of the important issues in predicting success in marriage concerns not only the psychological leaving of home, but also the nature of the parental marriage. When parental marriages do not function well, a psychological split develops between husband and wife. Even if they have not divorced, the split poses great problems for one or more of the children. If barriers develop in the relationship and bitterness sets in, the partners' usually unconscious choosing of a child as a "substitute mate" means that the child is going to develop a strong attachment to the parent. This may hinder, if not cripple, the child's ability to find a suitable mate and to maintain that relationship. The parental marriage has great importance as a model for the young couple, whether it is healthy or psychologically split.

During the wrap-up, the counselor should describe the nature of the parental marriage with the couple, as well as the family interactional style in terms of flexibility and connectedness. Counselors who use the PREPARE inventory can incorporate into the wrap-up the material from the inventory, including the family dynamics of flexibility and closeness.

When the counselor presents the wrap-up on the family of origin, he or she should address the discussion to the partner who is marrying into that family. For example, the counselor should direct to Mary a description of John's family of origin. If the counselor describes John's family of origin to him, he may either defend the material or be preoccupied with relating to the counselor. If the counselor talks to Mary about John's family of origin, John is able to listen and free his mind to absorb what is being said. John should be included in the discussion as the "consultant" about his family of origin, which helps him take a look as a "new outsider" and gain a perspective that appropriately differentiates him from his family. Then, the counselor would use the same method in describing Mary's family to John, with Mary as the consultant. Finally, there would be a discussion between Mary and John with the counselor as the facilitator.

Part 3a: Parents Attend a Session (Optional)

We have added to the FOE an optional session that has to do with bringing both sets of parents into the last session with the premarital or remarital couple. This may be impossible to do because of geographical distances between the couple and parents, or it may not be something that the counselor wishes to do with a particular couple. Even though the following description assumes that each partner's parents are still married to each other, we have also found the parental session to work well when the parents are divorced or widowed and when only one parent can therefore attend.

Rationale for Including Parents

The premarital or remarital counselor does not have a contract to work with the parents on their marriages. He or she can, however, have the young couple invite the parents to the last session. If the counselor wishes to include parents or stepparents in the final stage of counseling, we suggest that he or she inform the couple of this intention during the first session of the counseling process and explore the possibility of its happening. Not only is it important for the premarital or remarital couples to know ahead of time, but it is also important for them to be coached by the counselor in how to present the invitation to the parents. They can be instructed to indicate to the parents that marriage is a very special and meaningful event in their lives. As young people, they are making a step like the one their parents made many years ago. The invitation to the parents helps them to connect with and celebrate this event in the lives of their children.

Conducting the Parental Session

We suggest that when the parents arrive for the session, the counselor begin by explaining why they were asked to come. In this explanation, the premarital or remarital counselor can talk about the theory of parental models. The point of this brief introduction is not to underscore any difficulty the children may have with leaving home, but rather to emphasize the concept that parents are indeed important models for children. The counselor explains that the bride and groom have observed sometimes without consciously knowing it their parents' marriages of eighteen, twenty, or however many years, and that these four people, as objects of such observation, have been teaching their young people about marriage and family life.

As part of the explanation to parents, the counselor also can say, in the presence of all six, that he or she has discovered that most parents have had their own struggles with trying to carve out a successful marriage, especially in their early years. He or she can add that each marriage requires adjustment; some marriages need more adjustment than others.

Last, the counselor can indicate that the parents will no longer have the same kind of access to their children after the marriage as before. Here, the counselor can underscore that marriage is a developmental milestone. Marriage changes the way people relate to each other. Not only does it alter the way a man and woman relate to each other, but it also changes the way parents relate to their adult children. Marriage is a kind of passage into adulthood, a milestone in the maturing process. While children are single, parents frequently feel they can offer the children plentiful advice. Once a child makes the move to marriage, that child is in effect saying to parents, "I am becoming an adult. I am going to do the very same things you do." Although not all people experience marriage as the passage to adulthood, it is still valuable for the counselor to stress the importance of marriage as a developmental milestone; this will help the generations separate. All of this is a way of saying that with the marriage of their children, parents are experiencing a kind of loss. Children are also experiencing a kind of loss. Marriage marks a passage of time.

The focus of the session with the parents is an attempt to wrap up not only the changing nature of the parent-child relationship, but also the passing on of marital and family wisdom. The counselor should indicate to the parents that in this setting, they are being asked to give their children a last piece of wisdom. Each will have his or her time to talk. In one sense, this is their opportunity to say good-bye to their child as a single person, and to say hello to the marital couple. The counselor can aid the parents by posing two questions. First, what piece of advice would they give their child about how to succeed in marriage—advice they learned in their own marriage? Second, how are they going to continue their own marriage now that the child is moving on? How will their relationship now be different?

We think the counselor should structure that part of the session, rather than turn it over to the family. It is helpful for the counselor to provide structure for the rest of the session, as well. Indicate which parents should speak first; if one couple needs more time to think, go to the other. The counselor has the responsibility of keeping the session moving, but the parents, and to some degree their children, have the responsibility of doing the talking. When the parents have finished with what they have to say, the counselor can summarize what the parents said as a way of recapping and heightening both the happiness and the poignancy of this session.

The participants in the session with the parents will probably experience it as somewhat strange and tense, but it will be rewarding for a counselor who has not had the opportunity to go through this process before. The more such sessions that the counselor conducts, the more efficient and successful they will become. It is important to note that if the counselor is enjoying the task and having fun, the couple and the parents will, too—and they will benefit more from the process.

Part 4: The Premarital Inventory

In the previous chapter, we pointed out that an assessment inventory is a very useful part of the premarital and remarital counseling process. While the process that we present in this book could be done without an inventory, we believe that the process would be much inferior to that which uses an inventory. By using an inventory along with the DRH and FOE, the counselor has a wealth of information with which to provide an effective and influential counseling experience. An inventory also provides information from another point of view, that is, each partner's response to standardized questions; when these responses are scored in categories, the counselor can use them for a normative understanding of the couple. This information is different from the interview process, which captures the couple's verbal descriptions about themselves and their relationship through the methods of the DRH and FOE.

Both are crucial for the total premarital and remarital counseling process.

Information from a premarital or remarital inventory is used throughout the counseling sessions as a source of direct feedback, as a way to focus and enhance discussions of topics, and as a basis for skill building in such areas as communication, decision making, conflict resolution, budgeting, and so forth. We will say more about premarital and remarital inventories in the next chapter.

Part 5: Wedding Preparation

The purpose of Part 5 in our counseling process is to focus on the special role and task of clergy in the wedding itself. However, we believe that the information and ideas presented will also be useful to the nonclergy counselor in heightening awareness of religious issues and topics.

We assume that clergy will routinely discuss with the couple the mechanics of the wedding and the reception, the meaning of the various parts of the wedding service, and any other liturgical considerations. Some clergy will involve the couple in writing some or all of the service. Others will prefer to follow established liturgies. In either case, couples are likely to appreciate the service more if they understand it fully.

Every pastor confronts the issues of whether or not to include religious or theological issues in the premarital and remarital counseling process and if so, what kind. We will now present two approaches to including specifically religious or theological issues.

Method 1

One method of approaching such issues is to integrate them into the counseling process. This method does not use a specific, formal discussion. Nor does it lecture on the theology of marriage or on the nature and meaning of marriage within the perspective of faith. It does not present the established theological perspective of the denomination or of the pastor. Rather, Method 1 focuses on the couple and on helping them become aware of: (1) each person's religious belief system, (2) the similarities and differences in their religious value systems, (3) each person's practice of their faith, (4) the similarities and differences in their religious practices, and (5) their future plans regarding their religious practices. Method 1 aims to heighten each partner's awareness of the other person's uniqueness, to enhance their enjoyment of the values and practices they share, and to increase their respect for each other's beliefs and plans for practicing them in the future.

The approach of Method 1 has already been integrated into the outlined counseling process. For our purpose here, we want to highlight this approach. When we described the DRH, we suggested exploring the area of religion and religious practice. As described in Chapter Four, clergy have an excellent opportunity to focus on both religious values and religious practice at this point in the process. If that suggestion is followed as outlined, the result should be a clarification of who these two people are in regard to their religious orientation and practice. When describing the FOE, we recommended an exploration of the parents' religious orientations and practices and the kinds of models they provided in this area. If the FOE in this area is followed as outlined earlier in this chapter, the couple should develop a heightened awareness of both their differences and their similarities.

When partners have pronounced differences, the prescribed sections of the DRH and FOE should help them appreciate those differences. However, clergy can also help the couple develop respect for their differences and begin to negotiate a resolution to any conflict those differences produce.

Several concepts are implicit in Method 1. First, the focus is on the couple—not on the institution—and where they are coming from and going to, religiously speaking. Second, the purpose of premarital and remarital counseling is to explore and enhance the new relationship. Concern for the spiritual dimension of the individuals and the relationship is an ongoing pastoral theme and covers the entire life span of the individuals and the couple. The relationship, then, takes primary focus during counseling, whereas spiritual growth becomes more important in groups for married couples, retreats, enrichment programs, and other religious education experiences.

Third, the DRH and FOE implicitly have a deeply theological task. The second chapter of the book of Genesis addresses the nature of the man-woman relationship: "It is not good that man should be alone; I will make him a helper fit for him." Although many have incorrectly interpreted the word helper to mean "help-mate," it would be better translated "another human being like or corresponding to him." The original Hebrew says "another person (woman) to live alongside him." This passage thus suggests that a man shall leave his parents and take a wife. That is, they shall live alongside each other. They shall have a bond between them greater than the bond that each has with his or her parents. When the Genesis account says that a man and a woman become one flesh, it means that a husband and wife create a new home, sepa-rate from their parents, a home from which their own children will leave. The man and woman are to marry each other, not their par-ents or their children. The DRH and FOE are designed to deal with the important process of life's pilgrimage in a familial and psy-chological sense, but also in a deeply theological one.

Method 2

The other method of approaching religious or theological issues involves adding a separate unit to the premarital and remarital counseling process. Method 2 has two focuses: helping the couple explore and expand the spiritual dimension of their relationship, and formally discussing or presenting the meaning of marriage from a perspective of faith. Ministers may choose one or both of these.

Clergy who wish to present a formal discussion or lecture on the theology of marriage can present either their own theological or scriptural understanding or their denomination's interpreta-tion. We are not going to develop a theology of marriage here. There are too many differing theological and denominational perspectives to encompass. Ministers should, however, have little difficulty in finding ample material in their libraries or from de-nominational resources.

The separation of Part 4 into two methods is not meant to imply that clergy cannot borrow from both methods. Methods 1 and 2 can be put together. Clergy will need to settle issues of em-phasis and time management.

Part 6: Postwedding Session (Bonus)

We have found that a session with the couple six months after the wedding has been very helpful and valuable. By that time, the couple has been living together as a married couple long enough to have confronted the differences that appear during day-to-day life. Many of the issues that seemed more abstract during the prewedding sessions are often now real and vivid.

It is our suggestion that the appointment be set up at the time of the last prewedding session and then that a reminder be sent to the couple just prior to the session. Our experience indicates that a high number of the couples not only keep the appointment but find the sessions most profitable.

This postwedding session can also provide the counselor with feedback on the counseling process. What was useful to the couple about counseling? Were various units or components such as the DRH, FOE, skill-building and review exercises, and the premarital counseling inventory helpful? Were there topics or issues that were not covered and that might be included for other couples? Here, the counselor is doing not just a customer satisfaction survey, but in fact is doing research on the outcome of his or her counseling process.

The content of the postwedding session can be based on a review of the dimensions of marriage that were discussed in Chapter Two. Also, some of the areas identified in the premarital inventory can be reviewed. Often, as the counselor and couple discuss "How has it been to be married these six months?" the focus for this session emerges. At the conclusion of the session, the counselor can suggest that at some future date the couple participate in a marital enrichment retreat as a means of keeping their marriage alive and in tune.

In this chapter, we have completed our presentation of the procedure for premarital and remarital counseling. We have presented in detail the methodology for doing the Family of Origin Exploration (FOE), which is a structured way of assessing the client's family context, looking at such things as parental models and parent-child interaction. We have suggested that the counselor consider inviting the clients' parents to a session as a means of saying goodbye to their children as single persons and hello to the married couple, and we have suggested that the counselor schedule a session with the couple six months after the wedding. We have also introduced the advantage of using assessment inventories, which will be detailed in the next chapter.

Chapter Six

Premarital and Remarital Counseling Inventories

In this chapter, we wish to consider assessment inventories that both clergy and nonclergy counselors can use. The instruments and assessment inventories discussed here are appropriate for either conjoint couple or group premarital and remarital counseling.

The Nature of Assessment Inventories

In our discussion, we have deliberately chosen to use the more broadly based terms *assessment inventories* and *instruments,* rather than the frequently used word *test.* Our purpose in selecting the broader terms is to underline that the various approaches to assessment in premarital and remarital counseling cover a broad range, including specific forms such as questionnaires, personality inventories, psychological tests, rating scales, personal data forms, and other types of published material. Counselor training, approach, and the context of the counseling all influence whether assessment inventories are used, and which ones may be preferred. In our research on premarital and remarital counselors, we found that the majority of them used some assessment instruments in their work, and that those who did so rated themselves as more competent counselors than those who did not use them.[1]

When used appropriately, well-designed and carefully developed inventories can greatly benefit both the couple and the counselor. It is the responsibility of each counselor to determine whether or not a specific assessment instrument or inventory is appropriate for use with a particular couple or group. Also, the counselor must determine whether or not the inventory seems to provide accurate and meaningful information. Counselors must not erroneously assume that just because an assessment inventory has been published or made available for use, it is always suitable. Thus we call for the judicious selection of assessment inventories prior to their use in premarital and remarital counseling. We now discuss specific criteria to aid the counselor in evaluating inventories.

Considerations in Using Premarital and Remarital Inventories

In addition to the rather obvious issue of whether or not assessment inventories are compatible with the goals and procedures of the counseling process, there are a number of other important considerations.

Training and Background

People with a master's degree in counseling will probably have taken a course in assessment as part of their graduate work. We believe that such a course provides very useful background for the appropriate use of assessment inventories in counseling. Clergy, who may not have had graduate study in assessment, may wish to complete such a course at a nearby college. Before a counselor can purchase and use the inventories we discuss—PREPARE, PREPARE-MC, and MATE, which are published by Life Innovations—he or she must attend a daylong training workshop or complete self-study video training. Life Innovations will provide a current list of available training workshops.[2]

Evaluating Inventories

Counselors must have studied and taken any assessment inventory themselves before they attempt to use that inventory with couples. Assuming that the counselor has some background and training in assessment, we suggest that he or she take the following steps when considering a specific inventory for use.

- Obtain a specimen set (sample) of the instrument from the publisher. The specimen set typically contains an abbreviated copy of the instrument manual, the question booklet, the instrument answer sheets, scoring keys, and profile sheets or report forms.

- Study these materials.
- Take the inventory.
- Administer the inventory to another person whom the counselor knows well: a spouse, a close friend of the opposite sex, or someone else of significance to the counselor.
- Read the manual to find out how to score and profile the instrument, or send the instrument to the computer scoring service to be scored.
- Read the manual to understand and interpret the information the instrument provided. Interpret what the instrument reported about the counselor and the other person.
- Discuss the results and the process of taking the instrument with the other person. Evaluate whether the instrument was obtrusive or upsetting to take. Evaluate the ease and clarity of scoring and interpreting the results.
- Evaluate whether the scores and information provided by the instrument make sense to both people. Do the results support or contradict what the counselor knows about himself or herself and the other person?
- Assuming that the instrument looks appropriate up to this point, administer it to several other couples whom the counselor knows well, in an attempt to get their reactions to the process and to validate or document the accuracy of the information that the instrument yields.
- Re-administer the instrument to the counselor and the first person about two weeks after the initial administration. Score and interpret the results. Compare the earlier results with the current ones and note any changes that have occurred. Are the results consistent and still meaningful? Of course, we realize that by now the counselor is likely to be somewhat biased, because after having recently taken and studied the instrument, the counselor is very familiar with the construction and purpose of the instrument. However, taking it again can help the counselor look at the reliability and stability of the assessment over a short period of time and see what factors might affect the results.

- Assuming that the instrument has satisfied the counselor, he or she can begin to use it in counseling. Because the information gained from the assessment inventory will be used in combination with other information, the counselor can continually monitor and validate the data that it provides in the counseling process.

It is obvious that the process just described will need to be modified a bit, depending on the specific nature of the instrument or inventory being evaluated. For example, in assessing an open-ended questionnaire or personal data blanks, the counselor would not follow all of the steps as outlined. However, we cannot stress the point too strongly: *a counselor must always personally take an assessment inventory or complete a questionnaire before asking a client couple to do so.*

Advantages and Disadvantages of Assessment Inventories

There are advantages as well as disadvantages to using assessment inventories in premarital and remarital counseling. Generally, the use of paper-and-pencil assessment inventories is warranted and justified; however, there will be times when the counselor will appropriately choose not to use such aids. Our idea here is to determine whether or not the counselor will use paper-and-pencil assessment inventories. We believe it is safe to assume that even though counselors may choose to exclude such inventories from the counseling process, they will be using informal and subjective clinical assessment as part of the process.

Advantages

There are several advantages to using inventories in premarital and remarital counseling. First, instrumentation will promote a higher level of couple involvement and investment in the counseling process. By adequately explaining the rationale for using assessment inventories and pointing out in general terms what information will be obtained, the counselor enlists a strong commitment from the couple to use the assessment process and to try to understand its results. This commitment can further enhance the counseling process and outcome.

Second, inventories can elicit information that would take hours to obtain through interviewing. The couple can complete the assessment inventory outside the session and save precious counseling time. To ensure that the couple's experience in taking the inventory is as positive as possible, we suggest that they complete the inventory in the counseling office and not take it home. This is also helpful because any questions can be answered, the counselor is assured of correctly completed answer sheets, and the inventory booklet and answer sheet copyright are protected.

Third, inventories ensure that the counselor will obtain information from the couple, and for the couple, about the multidimensional aspects of their perceptions, beliefs, and backgrounds. For example, there are assessment inventories of various types that can assist in eliciting information about knowledge, attitudes, personality dynamics, life values, behaviors, and experiences.

Fourth, depending on the instrument used, inventories can provide the counselor and couple with useful normative information. It is useful to have accurate data or information on some aspects of personal and interpersonal behavior in order to compare the couple with other groups included in the normative samples reported in inventory manuals. It has been established that a valid assessment inventory will provide the counselor with a more accurate basis for such comparisons than subjective clinical judgment.

Fifth, in recent years, assessment inventories have been the bases for descriptions of couple types and patterns reported and discussed in the counseling literature. These couple types can be very useful to the counselor in understanding the couple and in providing feedback and information to the couple during the counseling process.

The final advantage of using assessment inventories in counseling is often overlooked: they can provide the couple with longitudinal data about themselves, and can give the counselor information about the counseling provided. Assessment data gathered at one time can be compared with data gathered at another time. For example, inventories can be taken twice during counseling in order to document or assess change. Or inventories can be taken during premarital or remarital counseling and then again after the wedding. Many couples have found it useful to go back to the premarital inventories and questionnaires to look at how they responded then and compare that to the results of the inventories after marriage. Examining the changes in the relationship in this way is helpful, whether the couple is looking at changes in relation to marital problems or in terms of marital enrichment. This also gives the counselor information that he or she can use to examine, and possibly modify, the counseling process and outcome.

Disadvantages

One disadvantage of using assessment inventories in premarital or remarital counseling is that it is possible for couples to misunderstand the intent of the process. Assessment inventories may instill in the couple the fear that there is something wrong with them or that they are troubled in their relationship. However, we believe that this disadvantage can easily be overcome if the counselor carefully explains the reasons for using assessment inventories and the potential information to be gained from them.

A second disadvantage might be that the counselor could tend to label or categorize the couple. Certainly, the information that many inventories yield involves specific names, patterns, or types, and therefore could lead to labeling or categorization. However, such a result would be the fault of the counselor, not the inventory. The use of information is solely the responsibility of the counselor. The skillful counselor will not use the information from an assessment inventory for labeling and categorization, but will interpret the information with the couple so that they can come to a better understanding of themselves and their relationship.

A third disadvantage is that the counselor could use the inventory results as the primary or only information conveyed to the couple about their relationship and themselves. In other words, the counselor can become "test-tied," using the inventory as a crutch, sticking closely to the interpretation of the data as the primary or exclusive focus of counseling. To do so is obviously inappropriate, because reporting or interpreting the results of the inventory alone is not counseling. The inventory is a supplement to counseling, not a replacement for the counseling process.

Counselors can likely find additional advantages and disadvantages of instrumentation in the premarital and remarital counseling process. Our purpose is to highlight the major pros and cons so that counselors might evaluate how inventories or assessment methods could strengthen their counseling.

Guidelines for Using Inventories with Clients

A number of relevant guidelines for the appropriate use of inventories in human relations training and general counseling have emerged over the years. We present these suggestions here.

It is the responsibility of the counselor to justify the use of the assessment inventory or instrument to the couple. The clients need to understand why they are being asked to complete the instrument. To respond to this concern, the counselor should explain to the couple that the instrument will yield information that will serve as an adjunct or supplement to the interview, or will provide information from another frame of reference. The counselor must also be sensitive to the clients' possible anxieties about the assessment inventory and attempt to help the couple deal with those anxieties if they should arise. In order to do this, the counselor must know the inventory well.

Another very important guideline for the counselor is to assure the couple that they have control over their own assessment or inventory data. The counselor must describe in careful and concrete terms his or her policies and practices, as well as any particular legal requirements, regarding confidentiality of assessment data. This also applies to the confidentiality of the overall counseling process and any notes or records that the counselor will keep. The counselor must underscore the point, in keeping with professional ethical codes of conduct and state statutes, that no information concerning the counseling, including assessment inventories, will be reported or released to anyone without clients' written permission.

Counselors must be aware of and follow copyright laws. Most inventories are copyright protected, which means that no one can photocopy assessment inventories, booklets, answer sheets, and such. Clients generally should not be given assessment inventories to complete at home, nor should they be provided with written copies of the assessment results, unless the results are specifically designed for the couple to keep. The counselor summarizes the assessment information for the couple as an integral part of the counseling process, but the raw data (answer sheet, profile, and so forth) are for the counselor's eyes only. From professional and legal points of reference, assessment information is the property and responsibility of the counselor. Of course, it is appropriate for the couple to take notes on inventory results as discussed in counseling sessions or to make notes in and use material such as *Building a Strong Marriage Workbook,* which is provided to couples who take inventories such as PREPARE and PREPARE-MC.

The counselor needs to make a conscious effort to uncover any mystery surrounding the assessment inventories that the client senses. The counselor can do this before they complete the inventory by briefly discussing what the inventory can and cannot provide. In the session after they take the inventory, the counselor should ask the couple about their reactions to taking the instrument and deal with those feelings. The counselor might ask, "What was your reaction to taking the inventory? Do you have any questions about it?" We feel that the counselor should discuss the idea that even though inventories are generally reliable over time— meaning that the same approximate scores or answers will be obtained with the same inventory at different times—the scores or data are not absolute. They are a "snapshot" of the couple's perceptions at the time they completed the inventory, and are therefore subject to some change.

The counselor needs to provide sufficient time for the couple to process and understand completely the inventory results. Depending on how the instrument is used in the counseling process, the nature of the inventory, and the dynamics of the couple, we find that some couples will need more time than others to discuss, understand, and apply assessment information to their situation.

Desirable Traits in Inventories

Several traits or characteristics of assessment inventories help counselors decide whether to use them. We offer a list of those characteristics to help the counselor make that choice. Counselors should ask themselves the following questions:

Is the information derived from the inventory necessary and appropriate for the counseling goals and purposes? For example, many personality tests do not lend themselves to premarital or remarital counseling because they are designed to measure certain personality traits and diagnose various types of mental illness. If we assume that the typical premarital or remarital client is not similar to a psychiatric patient, such inventories and the information obtained from them are not useful in this counseling process.

Is the inventory unobtrusive, or does it interfere with the counseling process? Our goal is to select and use inventories that blend with the counseling process and that the couple sees as a part of that process.

Is the inventory compatible with the orientation of the counselor? From the standpoint of the counselor, the design of the assessment inventory, the manner in which it is administered, and the tasks and questions it raises are all important considerations. For example, if the counselor's primary goal and theoretical orientation are for the couple to interact with each other rather than to focus on their individual traits and characteristics, assessment inventories that focus on the individual rather than the relationship would be inappropriate.

Does the inventory have a relationship and couple focus? Because the couple is the focus, information that can help the couple assess their interactional dynamics and their relationship must be provided. Of the thousands of assessment inventories and instruments published, relatively few have this interactional dimension. Therefore, if such nonrelational instruments are used, it is necessary for the counselor to extrapolate relationship and interactional information from them.

Can the couple understand the inventories easily? The clients must understand both why they are investing time in completing the inventories and the data and information that the inventories yield. Many questionnaires are self-explanatory and the information is readily understood. But is the information meaningful and understandable from the couple's point of view? It is important that the assessment inventories convey useful information and that this information is not misunderstood or threatening.

Are the inventories economical? The inventories must be reasonable from a monetary cost standpoint. They must also be economical in terms of the time commitment involved in completing and scoring them.

Relationship Assessment Inventories

PREPARE (from PREmarital Personal And Relationship Evaluation), PREPARE-MC (from PREmarital Personal And Relationship Evaluation—Marriage with Children), ENRICH (from ENriching Relationship Issues, Communication, and Happiness), and MATE (from Middle Age Transition Evaluation) are inventories that Dr. David Olson and colleagues at the University of Minnesota have developed and that Life Innovations has published. PREPARE is designed for use with couples who plan to marry and who have no children. PREPARE-MC is for engaged couples who have children. MATE is designed for older couples (fifty years or more) planning to marry or in marriage counseling, or couples facing other life transitions (retirement, relocation). ENRICH is designed for married couples seeking relationship enrichment or counseling and for couples who have cohabited for two or more years.[3]

The *PREPARE/ENRICH Counselor's Manual* points out several features of the inventories. They include the following criteria, which are important to the premarital and remarital counselor: a systemic theoretical base; a focus on issues relevant to couples in different stages, as the earlier inventory descriptions indicate; and a sound scientific and research base, meaning high reliability and validity, ability to discriminate happy from unhappy couples, and comparison with national norms. The inventories are designed to be practical and useful to counselors and couples.

As longtime users of these inventories, we would note that the support materials for the counselor, including the *Counselor's Manual,* computer-generated Counselor's Report of the couple's scores for use with the couple, *Counselor's Feedback Guide,* and *Building A Strong Marriage Workbook* are all very user-friendly, thorough, and well done. All of these materials were revised in 1996.

In the following discussion, we will look at PREPARE in detail, as one example of these inventories. Our goal is to overview the inventory so that the counselor can see the value of routinely including such an inventory in the counseling process. It is not our intent, nor is it possible, to have the reader become so acquainted with the inventory that she or he can use it in counseling. To achieve that, the counselor must attend a workshop for further training.

PREPARE

The PREPARE Inventory has 165 questions, including 30 background and demographic questions. The inventory was significantly revised in 1996, and over 40 percent of the current version is new, with another 32 percent having been revised from the earlier edition. PREPARE is designed to identify and measure premarital "relationship strengths" and "growth areas" in eleven categories. The inventory also contains (1) an idealistic distortion scale, which corrects the respondent's tendency to answer the items in an idealistic way; (2) scores describing the closeness and flexibility of both the couple's relationship and their families of origin; (3) four personality scales; and (4) an analysis of the couple as belonging to one of four premarital couple types.

It takes the typical person approximately thirty to forty minutes to complete the inventory. PREPARE must be scored by a computer, which provides a very useful report and interpretive aids for the counselor to use.

The respondent also provides very useful background information, including such things as age; education completed; employment; occupation; religion; ethnicity; annual income; how many years the partners have known each other; how many months remain before the wedding; whether the woman is pregnant; the number of children desired; how long after the wedding the partners want to begin having children; the parents' reaction to the marriage; friends' reaction to the marriage; parents' marital status; birth position or birth order; number of siblings; population of the place of current residence and of residence during childhood; whether the partners have ever broken up; whether parents or respondents had problems with alcohol or drug use; whether respondents observed parental abuse (verbal, emotional, or physical); whether respondents were ever abused (verbally, emotionally, physically, or sexually) by parents, partner, or anyone; and how often the respondent currently feels happy and enjoys life.

Content Areas

The descriptions of the eleven PREPARE content areas (scales) are reported in the *Counselor's Manual* and are summarized as follows:

1. *Marriage expectations.* This scale assesses a person's expectations about love, commitment, and conflict in his or her relationship. As the scale name implies, the goal is to assess the degree to which expectations about marriage are realistic and based on objective reflection.

2. *Personality issues.* This scale assesses a person's perception of his or her satisfaction with his or her partner in regard to such traits as tardiness, temper, moodiness, stubbornness, jealousy, and possessiveness. Personal behaviors related to public demonstration of affection and use of chemical substances are assessed. It also considers a partner's general outlook, dependability, and tendency to be domineering.

3. *Communication.* This scale measures the individual's feelings, beliefs, and attitudes toward the role of communication in the relationship. The items in this scale focus on the level of comfort each partner feels in being able to share emotions and beliefs with one another, the perception of the partner's listening and speaking skills, and the perception of the communication level in the relationship.

4. *Conflict resolution.* This scale assesses the partner's attitudes, feelings, and beliefs about the existence and resolution of conflict in the relationship. As with other scales, specific behaviors are assessed, which can be useful for feedback to the couple in the counseling process.

5. *Financial management.* This scale assesses the partners' attitudes and concerns about the way economic issues are managed in the relationship. Items assess such things as the partners' tendencies to be spenders or savers, awareness and concern about credit and debt, and wisdom of financial choices.

6. *Leisure activities.* This scale assesses attitudes and preferences for spending leisure time actively or passively with or without the partner.

7. *Sexual relationship.* This scale assesses the individual's feelings and concerns about affection and the sexual relationship with the partner. Items ask about affection, sexual behavior, family planning, and the ability to discuss such topics.

8. *Children and parenting.* This scale assesses attitudes and feelings about having and rearing children, including issues such as family size and the impact of potential children on the marital relationship.

9. *Family and friends.* This scale assesses each partner's feelings and perceptions about relationships with relatives, in-laws, and friends. Items focus on attitudes of family and friends toward the marriage, expectations about the amount of time to be spent with family and friends, and so forth.

10. *Role relationship.* This scale evaluates an individual's beliefs, feelings, and attitudes about marital and family roles. This scale has an implied bias toward egalitarian role behaviors.

11. *Spiritual beliefs.* This scale assesses the partner's attitudes, feelings, and concerns about the meaning of religious beliefs and practices within the context of the relationship.

PREPARE also assesses the closeness and flexibility of the current couple relationship and the families of origin. These scales are provided as content areas or scales on the Counselor's Report and are also plotted on an attached graph of the Couple and Family Map. An example of the Couple and Family Map from *Building a Strong Marriage Workbook* appears in Figure 6.1.

For each of the eleven categories, the PREPARE Counselor's Report presents the inventory items score for the partners. There is also a summary statement for the male and female, as well as the percentage of items on which the couple agreed and whether the area is a relationship strength or growth area. Special Focus items are items that the couple agrees are a problem in their relationship. For example, in Figure 6.2 both members of the couple have responded that they disagree by marking response 2, "I can express my true feelings to my partner." See Figure 6.2 for an example of the Counselor's Report for the Communication Scale. The reader can see that there is much information provided for use in premarital and remarital counseling.

Personality

The 1996 revision of PREPARE introduced the assessment of four personality traits. The *Counselor's Manual* states that the "personality assessment is designed to increase the premarital counselor's understanding of each partner and how these personality characteristics are related to the underlying couple dynamics. These four areas are interrelated with each other and together provide a rather comprehensive picture of each person."[4] The personality traits assessed are:

Figure 6.1. Couple and Family Map.

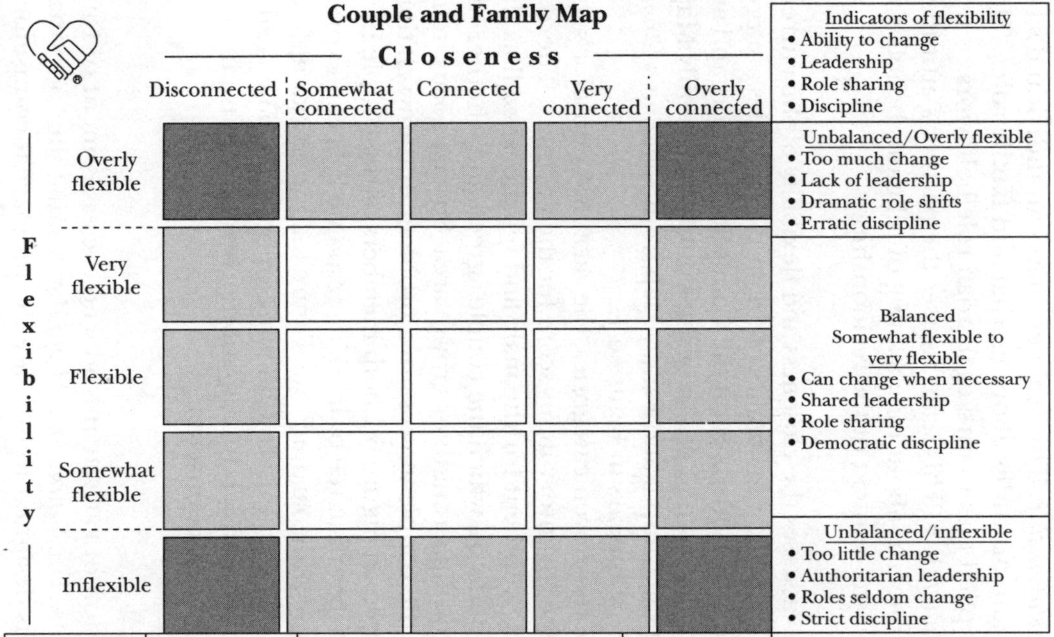

Couple and Family Map

C l o s e n e s s

	Disconnected	Somewhat connected	Connected	Very connected	Overly connected
Overly flexible					
Very flexible					
Flexible					
Somewhat flexible					
Inflexible					

(Row axis label: F l e x i b i l i t y)

Indicators of flexibility
- Ability to change
- Leadership
- Role sharing
- Discipline

Unbalanced/Overly flexible
- Too much change
- Lack of leadership
- Dramatic role shifts
- Erratic discipline

Balanced
Somewhat flexible to very flexible
- Can change when necessary
- Shared leadership
- Role sharing
- Democratic discipline

Unbalanced/inflexible
- Too little change
- Authoritarian leadership
- Roles seldom change
- Strict discipline

Legend:
- □ Balanced
- ▨ Mid-range
- ▦ Unbalanced

Indicators of closeness	Unbalanced Disconnected	Balanced Somewhat connected to very connected	Unbalanced Overly connected
Separateness (I) vs. togetherness (we)	Too much (I) separateness	Good I-we balance	Too much (we) togetherness
Closeness	Little closeness	Moderate to high closeness	Too much closeness
Loyalty	Lack of loyalty	Moderate to high loyalty	Loyalty demanded
Independence	High independence	Interdependent	High dependency

Source: From *Building a Strong Marriage Workbook: PREPARE/ENRICH Program,* 1996, Minneapolis, MN: Life Innovations. Reprinted by permission.

Figure 6.2. Sample Counselor's Report for Communication.

COMMUNICATION

The male has some concerns about their communication and is sometimes unable to share his feelings and be understood by his partner.
The female has some concerns about their communication and is sometimes unable to share her feelings and be understood by her partner.

Check items to discuss ✓	Agreement	Indecision	Disagreement	Special focus	M	F		☞®	Positive couple % 40%	Relationship strength or growth area — Possible growth area	Revised scores Male % 28%	Female % 16%
				S	2	2	(+)	3.	I can express my true feelings to my partner.			
			D		5	3	(−)	18.	When we are having a problem, my partner often refuses to talk about it.			
	A				1	2	(−)	33.	My partner sometimes makes comments that put me down.			
				S	4	5	(−)	48.	I wish my partner were more willing to share feelings with me.			
			D		2	4	(−)	63.	At times it is hard for me to ask my partner for what I want.			
	A				2	2	(−)	78.	Sometimes I have trouble believing everything my partner tells me.			
				S	4	5	(−)	93.	My partner often doesn't understand how I feel.			
	A				4	4	(+)	107.	I am very satisfied with how my partner and I talk with each other.			
			D		2	4	(−)	121.	It is difficult for me to share negative feelings with my partner.			
	A				5	4	(+)	134.	My partner is a very good listener.			

Source: From Sample Counselor Report: PREPARE/ENRICH Program, 1996, Minneapolis, MN: Life Innovations. Reprinted by permission.

Assertiveness: A person's ability to express feelings to his or her partner and be able to ask for what he or she would like.

Self-confidence: How good a person feels about himself or herself and about the ability to control things in life.

Avoidance: A person's tendency to minimize issues and the reluctance to deal with issues directly.

Partner dominance: How much a person feels his or her partner tries to control him or her and dominate their life.

This personality information is obviously valuable as a counselor conducts the DRH.

Couple Types

The 1996 revision of PREPARE and PREPARE-MC added a figure showing four types of premarital couples. The scores for the couple taking the inventory are reported on the computer-generated Counselor's Report so that the counselor can compare the client couple with the four premarital couple types. The report indicates which premarital type the couple is most similar to and also provides some suggestions for counseling that type of couple.

The four couple types are based on research with 4,618 couples who took PREPARE before marriage. The details of the study are reported in the *Counselor's Manual* and have been reported in journal articles and at professional meetings. The premarital couple types are as follows:

Vitalized couples have a high degree of agreement across the eleven dimensions assessed by PREPARE. They tend to have the happiest marriages and are the least likely to divorce.

Harmonious couples also tend to have high positive couple agreement on the PREPARE dimensions except in financial management and children and parenting. These couples tend to be happy and are at low risk for divorce.

Traditional couples tend to have lower agreement scores in interpersonal areas (communication, conflict resolution) but higher scores in the more traditional external areas (children and parenting, family and friends, spiritual beliefs). Few of these couples divorce, but while many stay together, they are rather unhappily married.

Conflicted couples have the lowest percentage of positive agreement scores of any premarital type. They tend to be at the highest risk for divorce and they are often unhappily married. The premarital couple types are shown in Figure 6.3.

The PREPARE manual is clearly written and contains excellent guidelines and instructions for administering and interpreting the instrument. The sections on administration and research have particular information addressed to clergy and religious settings, as well as to other uses. The PREPARE *Counselor Feedback Guide* is an outstanding aid, designed to assist the counselor in summarizing and organizing the information to discuss with the couple in feedback sessions. Three feedback sessions are suggested as outlined in the *Counselor Feedback Guide* shown in Figure 6.4.

The counselor will see that a wealth of information is available from the PREPARE Inventory. The information can be used well in the premarital counseling process that we have outlined. For example, the goals of the PREPARE Program, as shown on the *Counselor Feedback Guide* and in Figure 6.4, fit our model well. The three feedback sessions also shown on the *Counselor Feedback Guide* could be incorporated into the sessions that we have outlined as Part 4, the Premarital Inventory. Information from the Couple and Family Map could be included in our Part 3, the FOE. The background information from PREPARE can be used in Parts 1 and 2, the Introduction and the DRH.

Building a Strong Marriage Workbook is a newly revised booklet designed for the counselor to use in the feedback sessions and for the couple to take home. The booklet provides the couple with helpful ideas about marriage and with information from their PREPARE inventory. Also included are two communication exercises, an exercise and worksheet giving ten steps for resolving couple conflict, a financial budgeting exercise, a goal-setting exercise (for personal, couple, and family goals), and the Couple and Family Map. The counselor who uses the PREPARE Inventory and related materials will find that they encompass what the inventory developers have called the "PREPARE/ENRICH Program."

In order to use PREPARE, PREPARE-MC, and MATE appropriately and to purchase the inventories, the counselor must attend a one-day training workshop. These workshops are offered throughout the country by a network of trainers. Information about the workshops

Figure 6.3. Four Types of Premarital Couples.

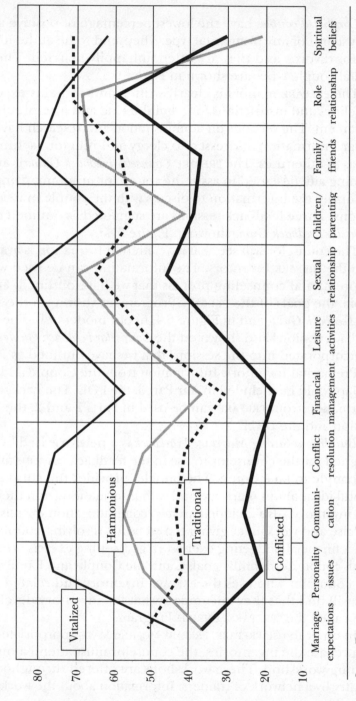

Source: From PREPARE/ENRICH *Counselor's Manual*, by D. H. Olson, 1996, Minneapolis, MN: Life Innovations. Reprinted by permission.

Figure 6.4. Counselor Feedback Guide.

Counselor feedback guide
PREPARE/ENRICH Program

Version
2000

Goals of the PREPARE/ENRICH program

◆Review these goals with the couple:
- Explore the couple's relationship strength and growth areas.
- Learn useful communications skills, including assertiveness and active listing.
- Learn skills to resolve conflicts through use of the ten steps procedure.
- Explore their couple relationship and their families of origin using the couple and family map.
- Develop their personal, couple, and family goals.
- Plan for the couple to review their marriage annually and attend couple enrichment programs.
- Develop financial plan and budget.

Feedback session 1

1. Review goals of the PREPARE/ENRICH program with the couple (see above).
2. Couple discusses their experience in taking the inventory.
3. Couple completes Couple Communication Exercise I.
4. Couple completes Couple Communication Exercise II.
5. Summarize session and review the ten steps procedure and assign it as homework for the couple.

Feedback session 2

1. Review couple's homework using ten steps for resolving couple conflict.
2. Counselor reviews communication (page 8 of the report) and conflict resolution (page 9 of the report) areas to identify strength (agreement items) and growth areas (special focus and disagreement items) with the couple.
3. Select one or two new issues (special focus or disagreement items) from any area to use with ten steps procedure.
4. Explore couple relationship and family of origin.
5. Summarize session and assign homework on financial plans and budget.

Feedback session 3

1. Review the homework assignment on financial plans and budget.
2. Have couple complete the goal exercise.
3. Summarize and discuss future goals.

Source: From *Counselor Feedback Guide: PREPARE/ENRICH Program,* 1996, Minneapolis, MN: Life Innovations. Reprinted by permission.

and PREPARE is available from the publisher (see Note 2 in the Notes for this chapter).

FOCCUS

Next to PREPARE, FOCCUS is probably the most widely used premarital and remarital counseling inventory that meets our criteria of being well designed and established. Since neither of the authors regularly uses FOCCUS, we invited our colleague, Lee Williams from the University of San Diego, to write this section.

FOCCUS (from Facilitating Open Couple Communication, Understanding and Study) is a premarital inventory that is widely used in the Catholic Church to prepare couples for marriage, but is also available in a nondenominational version for non-Catholic couples.[5] The FOCCUS inventory contains 156 items, with additional items for previously married couples, interfaith couples, and cohabiting couples.

FOCCUS was developed with four goals in mind. The first goal was to provide couples with objective criteria for assessing their relationship. FOCCUS items were written to reflect the current body of knowledge of what is necessary for a successful marriage. FOCCUS provides the couple with feedback on the preferred or most healthy response to each question.

The second goal was to address both contemporary and specialized needs of several couples. For example, FOCCUS includes questions that specifically address dual-career marriages, interfaith marriages, couples preparing for second marriages, as well as a new scale for cohabiting couples.

The third goal was to reflect the values and ideals of a sacramental marriage. These values and ideals include the permanence of marriage, fidelity, openness to having children, forgiveness, unconditional love, and a shared faith in God.

The fourth goal was to develop an instrument that would be user-friendly for both couples and counselors. The intent was to develop an inventory that did not require a highly trained professional to administer and interpret the test, yet had minimal risk for being misused.

The overall purpose of FOCCUS is to help couples learn more about themselves and their relationships. FOCCUS facilitates this process by providing couples with individualized feedback about where each partner stands in regard to several topics that are important to marriage. The feedback may point to topics or issues the couple has not discussed, or highlight areas of disagreement or concern that need to be addressed. The results of the inventory become a springboard for the couple to explore and discuss. They must decide how to best handle these important areas of their relationship. These areas include:[6]

Lifestyle expectations. Items in this category examine expectations of roles, expectations around the care and management of a household, and differences in goals and career plans.

Friends and interests. This category includes statements that explore possible conflicts over friends, conflicts over too little or too much closeness, and differences in interests.

Personality match. Items in this category help couples explore the degree to which their personalities are similar or different. Many of the items are based on the Myers-Briggs personality types. Items also explore the degree to which each partner respects and accepts the other's personality.

Personal issues. Statements in this category assess for personal problems that may cause conflicts in the relationship. For example, items address topics such as potential for alcohol or drug abuse, gambling, jealousy, and moodiness.

Communication. This category explores a variety of areas, such as listening and being able to comfortably share thoughts and feelings. It also assesses issues that frequently block communication, such as difficulty saying one is sorry or a desire to avoid conflict.

Problem solving. Items in this category explore the couple's ability and methods for problem solving. For example, statements examine the couple's ability to compromise and the way anger is handled in the relationship.

Religion and values. Items in this category examine the role of religion and values in the individual's life and in the couple's relationship. For example, some questions explore the degree to which religion strengthens or disrupts the relationship.

Parenting issues. Statements in this category examine expectations about having children, as well as possible negative attitudes or fears about parenting. For example, some statements explore the couple's openness to having children, as well as the number of children and the timing. In addition, there are items that assess expectations about parenting roles.

Extended family issues. This category has items that explore possible conflict with extended family, lack of acceptance or unease with the extended family, and significant differences in family background.

Sexuality issues. Items in this category assess for possible negative attitudes toward sexuality on the part of each individual, as well as possible problems or concerns regarding the sexual relationship.

Financial issues. Items in this category assess for concern over a partner's handling of money, possible conflict over financial roles or management, and potential financial hardships the couple may face.

Readiness issues. Items in this category assess for an individual's possible ambivalence about marriage or choice of partner, as well as pressures or objections to the marriage. Readiness issues also examine whether individuals have unrealistic expectations or a highly romantic view of marriage.

Marriage covenant. These items explore the degree to which the couple sees their relationship not just as a civil contract, but as a religious covenant where they "pledge to seek an uncompromising, limitless love for each other." Items in this category also explore the connection between the couple's marital and spiritual or church life.

Key problem indicators. The developers of FOCCUS have selected some inventory items from the preceding categories that they believe are often key indicators of problems in relationships. Two examples include: (1) "The use of some (alcohol/tobacco/marijuana/cocaine) causes problems between us, and (2) "The behavior of my future spouse sometimes frightens me."

Interfaith marriages. FOCCUS has eight items developed specifically for couples coming from different religious traditions. Statements in this category explore the degree to which religious differences may be a potential cause of conflict or lack of bonding. It also explores whether or not there is disagreement about the religious upbringing of children.

Second marriages. FOCCUS has nine items developed specifically for couples in which one or both partners have been previously married. Items explore a variety of issues, such as dealing with children from previous marriages and the impact of the previous marriages on the current relationship. The issues addressed include child support and alimony, disciplining of children, and possible troubles caused by an ex-spouse.

Cohabitation. The developers of FOCCUS have recently created and tested sixteen items designed specifically for cohabiting couples. The new items will be available in FOCCUS by January 1997. They explore areas such as the couple's decision to marry, expectations for marriage, attitudes about commitment, and the role of religion in the cohabiting couple's lives.

The predictive validity of FOCCUS has been demonstrated through empirical research,[7] and appears to be roughly comparable to that of PREPARE. Unfortunately, methodological differences between studies of FOCCUS and PREPARE do not allow for a head-to-head comparison. However, when extreme groups are compared, as was done in the PREPARE studies, the classification rates for FOCCUS are comparable to the rates quoted in the two PREPARE studies.

Although an instrument such as FOCCUS may be generally predictive of marital success with a group of couples, it does not correctly classify 100 percent of the couples. Therefore, instruments such as FOCCUS should never be used to predict whether or not individual couples will have a successful marriage, or to decide which couples should or should not marry. Using FOCCUS as a "pass-fail" test discourages couples from being truly open in discussing their relationship, the very process that FOCCUS was designed to facilitate.

The manual for FOCCUS states that most couples can complete the inventory in forty-five to sixty minutes. FOCCUS is available in a variety of forms to address the special needs of certain populations, such as those who speak Spanish or Castilian, those who read Braille, and those who do not read (they can use tapes).

A variety of options are available to the counselor for scoring FOCCUS. The developers of FOCCUS provide a computer scoring service. The fee for computer scoring is $10 and the developers promise a twenty-four-hour turnaround on scoring the instrument. FOCCUS is also available in a hand scoring format and can generally be scored this way in twenty to thirty minutes. A manual and disk for scoring FOCCUS on an IBM-compatible personal computer are available from Parish Data Systems.[8]

The FOCCUS manual can be quite helpful to counselors as they interpret and go over the results with the couple. The manual assists the counselor in identifying themes both within and across different topic areas. It also provides the counselor with questions he or she can ask to facilitate couple discussion. Finally, the manual supplies the counselor with suggested readings and resources for each topic area.

Taylor-Johnson Temperament Analysis

The Taylor-Johnson Temperament Analysis (T-JTA) is a measure of temperament and personality that has been widely used in premarital, remarital, marital, and family counseling. A feature that is unique to the T-JTA and that makes it particularly appropriate for use in premarital and remarital counseling is the crisscross testing. In the crisscross testing, a person takes the test first to describe himself or herself and then, on a separate answer sheet, completes the test again to describe the partner. Plotting one person's scores along with the scores of the partner's view generates very useful information and test profiles. Thus, for example, five profiles can be generated in the crisscross testing for a couple: (1) Robert as he described himself, (2) Joan as she described herself, (3) a combination profile showing how Robert described himself and how Joan described herself, (4) Robert as described by Joan, and (5) Joan as described by Robert.

The T-JTA is a 180–question instrument designed to measure nine bipolar personality characteristics. It requires approximately thirty to forty minutes to complete (double for crisscross administration) and approximately twenty minutes to score and profile the four answer sheets. Computer scoring service is available. Although the T-JTA is not designed to measure mental abnormalities in psychiatric terms, it does provide measures of temperament and personality patterns with sufficient validity and reliability for emotionally normal couples in a developmental-educational premarital and remarital counseling context. It also has the sensitivity to help identify persons who might benefit from additional individual or couple therapy.

The T-JTA's nine bipolar scales are used to assess the following personality or temperamental aspects in individuals: nervous versus composed, depressive versus lighthearted, active and social versus quiet, expressive and responsive versus inhibited, sympathetic versus indifferent, subjective versus objective, dominant versus submissive, hostile versus tolerant, and self-disciplined versus impulsive. In addition, there is a scale that indicates to the counselor the attitude of the person taking the test and how he or she wishes to be seen. A high score on the attitude scale suggests that the person taking the test has wanted to appear more admirable than he or she may actually be, whereas a low score suggests that the person has been overly critical of himself or herself.

T-JTA is a comprehensive instrument that is relatively straightforward and easy for couples to understand. The available profiles offer direct and concrete explanations of the temperament traits assessed. Profiles of couple types have been developed based on T-JTA profiles for use in premarital and marital counseling.[9] The instrument has been revised and new norms have been made available. Research literature reports ongoing studies with differing samples. The T-JTA manual is a model of thoroughness and completeness with counselors receiving periodic updates and supplements.

We believe that the use of assessment inventories, particularly those designed for use in premarital and remarital counseling, is an important part of the counseling process. The reader should now be able to apply appropriate criteria in selecting assessment inventories and evaluate the advantages and disadvantages of using them in counseling. We have discussed major inventories that, through years of development and refinement, have demonstrated their value when used in premarital and remarital counseling. In the next section, we will consider in detail special topics that are critical to providing premarital and remarital counseling.

Part Three

Special Topics

Chapter Seven

Remarriage and Stepparenting

As we point out in Chapter One, in nearly half of all weddings today, at least one partner has been married before. The most significant development in premarital and remarital counseling is the increasing number of remarriages today and the number of those couples who seek counseling before marriage. Approximately one-third of prewedding counseling is now done with remarital couples. Specifically, of the forty-six remarriages, eleven are a remarriage for the groom and another eleven are a remarriage for the bride. The remaining twenty-four are remarriages for both the bride and groom. Keep in mind that although the majority of persons remarrying had an earlier marriage end in divorce or annulment, these numbers also include widows and widowers.

In recent years, there has been a tremendous increase in professional and lay publications that focus on the problems of remarriage, particularly those involving the adjustments of divorced people and children to remarriage. The remarital and premarital counselor needs to be sensitive to the potential problems confronting those who wish to remarry. This chapter will examine two important topics—first, the general process of counseling for remarriage, and second, remarital counseling for stepparent couples, that is couples who will have children present from preceding relationships.

Theoretical Issues in Remarriage

It has been well established in family theory and family therapy theory that the degree of separation a person has from a previous marital relationship can be an important indicator of successful re-marriage. Before we move directly into the process of work with remarital couples, we will briefly note the theoretical issues that lie behind work with such couples.

Leaving the Previous Marriage

If a person has been married and that marriage has been termi-nated by death, divorce, annulment, separation, or desertion, the experience of that marital relationship will have a lasting impact on the person. We would agree with and expand upon the point made by Carl Whitaker and David Keith that a person cannot re-ally be psychologically divorced.[1] We believe that whatever causes a marriage to end, the partners can rarely completely get over or ignore the impact of that previous marital relationship. People are unable to dismiss significant intimate relationships from their life. Previous relationships have a significant impact on persons, and that impact may be positive or negative. Although it is possible to remove oneself physically from a relationship, it is rarely possible to remove every trace of that relationship so that a person is as he or she was prior to the time it began.

Decourting

Therapists speak of the decourting process, a divorce counseling process in which the goals are to help the partners get back as much of their original emotional and personal investment as pos-sible and to clarify practical factors, such as childrearing, in the new relationship. The task of the remarital counselor is to assist people in adequately resolving and dealing with their previous marital relationships. Even though the previous marriage may have been forgotten for the present time, or may perhaps have been sat-isfactorily discussed and resolved by the couple, the counseling process for remarriage should include a discussion of the experi-ence that each person had in a previous marriage and the impact on the current couple relationship.

Continuation of Previous Dysfunction

Often people voluntarily terminate marriages because of prob-lems, discomfort, or dysfunction in their particular relationship.

A counselor might expect, therefore, that people would carefully select a second marital relationship and prepare for it well so that the previous dysfunction might not be repeated. It would also seem that because a high percentage of divorced people tend to remarry, most people view marriage as a satisfying and valuable lifestyle. However, many people carry into a second marriage the problems, dysfunction, or hurt that they experienced in the first marriage.

In dealing with a remarriage, the counselor needs to be particularly alert to the probable reasons for the termination of the previous marriage. The counselor should help the couple assess the extent to which previous problems or dysfunctions have or have not been resolved. When such problems are found, the counselor must responsibly assist the individuals in resolving them or make an appropriate referral for such work. Such a remedial remarital counseling process often takes longer than the six- to eight-session remarital counseling process discussed in the earlier part of this book. The sessions may go on for several months, and may continue after the wedding.

Blaming Previous Relationships

It is not uncommon for persons who have been divorced to focus a great deal of blame on the previous marital relationship or previous spouse. Often the new partners see this as healthy, and can seem to strengthen the current relationship by downplaying the previous relationship. However, in the long run, such blaming is frequently dysfunctional. The task of the remarriage counselor, therefore, is to help the couple adequately differentiate the present marital relationship from the previous marital history, so that the couple can deal with the current relationship without needing to downplay the previous one.

Contexts of Remarriage Counseling

We believe that the context of remarital counseling shapes, to some degree, both the expectations of the remarital couple and the methodology of the remarriage counseling. We will look at the religious setting and the mental health clinic setting, which are common contexts for remarital and stepparent counseling.

Religious Setting

Although more first marriages take place in local religious settings than do remarriages, still a significant number of remarriages take place in the local congregation. We are not aware of any studies that compare and contrast couples who seek remarriage counseling from clergy versus from social service agencies. It is our suspicion, however, that couples who seek remarital counseling from their religious leader perceive the forthcoming remarriage in generally positive terms and have a minimal amount of concern regarding the success of the remarriage. This means that they generally are not approaching the remarital counseling with an orientation toward problems. Thus their expectations are somewhat similar to the couple approaching a first marriage, but not completely so.

Another factor affecting remarital counseling in church settings is that denominations may require remarital counseling before granting a church wedding. Couples approaching counseling in this context expect the clergy counselor not only to explore the current remarital relationship with an eye toward functionality, but also to pay attention to the dysfunction in the previous relationship and the possibility of its continuation in this current relationship. Thus, these couples expect scrutinization of the current and previous relationships. Many couples are cooperative and believe that the process is aimed toward helping them improve their relationship. But some couples are irritated and annoyed by the process and see it more as an obstacle than as an attempt to help improve their relationship.

Agency Setting

We have found that two types of remarital couples seek remarriage counseling from social service agencies and clinics: the previous client and the conflicted couple.

In some couples seeking remarital counseling in agency and clinic settings, one or both partners have had previous marital therapy. Sometimes the former clients return to the previous marital therapist, expecting the therapist to examine the current relationship to detect any signs of continuing dysfunction. Although the couple expectation in this situation is appropriate, many counselors functioning with a family therapy orientation would choose to refer this couple so that a new therapist with no previous alliance or relationship with the former client can begin working with the couple. In addition, it should be noted that many marital therapists working with a divorcing couple caution them about forthcoming relationships and may suggest remarital counseling to avoid perpetuating the dysfunction of the earlier marriage.

There are other couples who may or may not be former clients who are currently experiencing significant conflict in the prospective remarital relationship and are wondering whether they should terminate the relationship or go forward with the wedding. This couple expects the remarital counselor to help them explore the relationship, identify the cause of the dysfunction, and move toward some resolution. On occasion, counseling seriously conflicted remarital couples may seem more like marital therapy than remarital counseling. We will explore work with seriously conflicted couples in Chapter Eleven.

Design of Remarital Counseling

We have been suggesting our model of remarital counseling. As the reader has likely discovered from the previous chapters, there are many more similarities between remarital counseling and premarital counseling than differences. We will now briefly outline the design of remarital counseling and explore a number of administrative issues.

Administrative Issues

Although many of the administrative issues regarding remarital counseling are similar to those for premarital counseling, there are several specific issues that we need to consider.

Framework. In our remarital counseling model, the conjoint couple counseling process contains six basic units: introduction, DRH, exploration of previous marriages, FOE, wedding preparation, and postwedding session.

Sessions. The remarital counselor needs to make some decisions about the structure of the counseling sessions, particularly in regard to the length of each session and the number of sessions. The two-hour framework, as is typically employed in counseling couples preparing for first marriage, seems to be an appropriate model for remarital counseling as well. As to the number of sessions, we suggest at least five or six two-hour sessions for nonclergy. Clergy, who need to include theological and wedding material, would need to add another session. The discussion about contracting, fees, printed materials, and related matters in Chapter Three would apply to remarital counseling.

Remarital Inventory. In remarital counseling, we have found the use of a comprehensive inventory extremely valuable. Our preference is an inventory designed for couples in a prewedding situation that looks specifically at dimensions and topics related to remarriage and marriage. We feel that the best of these inventories are: (1) PREPARE-MC, which is designed for couples who are planning to marry and who already have children; (2) MATE, which is designed for older couples going through life transitions including marriage or remarriage; and (3) FOCCUS, which has a special section related to second marriages. Other instruments such as the Taylor-Johnson Temperament Analysis and the Myers-Briggs Type Indicator are useful personality inventories, but lack the scores and information directly related to marriage and remarriage. Most of these inventories were discussed in detail in Chapter Six.

Part 1: The Introduction

The introduction occurs at the beginning of the first session when the remarital counselor becomes acquainted with the couple. Part 1 of remarital counseling is identical to Part 1 of premarital counseling. All of the aspects discussed in Part 1 of Chapter Four apply to the remarriage counseling context, including the issues of getting acquainted, explanation of the process, instrumentation, and contracting.

Part 2: DRH

The second part of the remarital counseling process consists of an exploration of the current relationship from when the couple first met up to the proposed wedding, including the use of the DRH. In this sense, Part 2 of remarital counseling is identical to Part 2 of premarital counseling, in which couples prepare for their first marriage. Thus, the rationale for the DRH and the techniques for the DRH, as discussed in Part 2 of Chapter Four, apply in remarital counseling.

Areas of Focus

In conducting the DRH for remarital couples, the counselor can follow the process as previously presented, exploring the relationship from the time the couple first met until they began counseling. Through the use of the DRH, the remarital counselor can move through the history of the current relationship in a month-by-month fashion. All of the various themes and questions enumerated in Chapter Four about conducting the DRH also apply when conducting the DRH with remarital couples.

Prewedding Patterns

In working with remarital couples, the counselor is seeking clues about the nature of the current relationship and attempting to determine the kinds of patterns unfolding in the relationship. Thus, all of the themes mentioned in Chapter Four in "Interactional Patterns" will apply to the remarital couple. The counselor should observe themes and patterns such as commitment and bonding, dependency, self-esteem, communication patterns, power, intimacy, and religious practice. The counselor will want to include skill-building exercises from these topics in the several sessions devoted to this section of the counseling process.

The Wrap-Up

When the remarital counselor has completed the DRH, it is important that he or she spend time providing the couple with observations about the relationship. Remarital couples benefit enormously from an outsider's or third party's comments on their relationship. Thus, the remarital counselor can fashion the wrap-up in the same manner as with a couple preparing for their first marriage. We suggest including information gained from the inventory throughout the counseling sessions and during the wrap-up session.

Part 3: Exploration of Previous Marriages

In our model of remarital counseling, we place the examination of previous marriages after the exploration of the current relationship. This placement is designed to reduce the remarital couple's resistance. If the counselor begins by exploring previous relationships, rather than the current one, it generally irritates or upsets the couple. They have come to the counselor because of the current relationship, are usually excited and happy about the relationship, and have in some sense come to celebrate it. The current relationship is the relationship of primary importance. By attending to that one first, it is easier to move backward later and to explore previous marriages.

The purpose of Part 3 is to explore previous marriages in order to determine both the degree of resolution about those relationships and whether any dysfunctional patterns have continued in the current relationship. In many ways, Part 3 is similar to a DRH, although it is shorter and offers a more specific focus on determining the dynamics that brought about the previous marital breakdown.

Methodology

In exploring the previous marriage, we ask the couple to choose which partner wants to go first (provided both have been married previously). After the couple has chosen who will initiate the examination, we then focus primarily on that individual and his or her previous marriage. While conducting the exploration, we not only ask the individual to describe the previous marriage, but also ask the individual what the ex-partner would say to the questions as we go along the time line. This is a form of projective dyadic questioning as discussed in Chapter Four. In addition, if the prospective mate has some knowledge of the previous marriage, we invite that partner to add his or her observations as to the nature of the previous marriage. As in conducting the DRH, we make use of the time line and proceed in a linear fashion.

Areas of Focus

Although any of the areas of focus that were used with the DRH can be used in regard to previous marriages, we attempt to condense the previous marriage exploration by focusing on larger time frames, rather than going month by month. These will be evident in the areas of focus that follow.

Dating relationship. As in the DRH of the current relationship, we explore the dating relationship in the previous marriage, looking at it as an entire unit. We are interested in how the person perceived that dating relationship, what indications there are now, retrospectively, regarding the problems in the marriage. We ask about any peculiarities in the dating process, any items that now appear to be strange even though they were not perceived so at the time.

Beginning of conflict. Rather than moving through the time line month by month, we begin the marital portion by exploring the onset of conflict. We are interested in when the conflict began and how it manifested itself. In addition, we are interested in each partner's attempts either to manage or to resolve the conflict.

Attempts to change. As we move along the time line, we inquire about attempts to change the previous relationship, whether through professional counseling, through ideas generated by the couple, or by some other means.

Nature of the marital breakdown. We inquire as to the nature of the conflict, its ongoing manifestation, and the shape that the struggle began to take on in the relationship.

Decisions to separate and divorce. As couples move toward increasing marital conflict, it is not uncommon that they separate, come back together, separate, and ultimately divorce. We explore what precipitated the separation or the divorce, how the decision-making process evolved, who left the relationship first, and the actions of both mates in dealing with the decisions.

Process of parting. We are interested in how each of the former partners dealt with the pain of the separation and dissolving of the marital relationship. We are particularly interested in how each mate handled the pain of the divorcing process and whether either person sought any professional help at the time. In some remarital situations, the current relationship began as one or the other attempted to help the partner through the pain of a divorce. Thus, the current relationship may have evolved as a way of dealing with a previous marriage. If that is the case, we believe it is important to look at that pseudotherapeutic process and what it means for the current relationship, both now and in the future.

Similarities of relationships. After we have moved through the previous marriage, we want to look at the similarities between that earlier marital relationship and the current relationship. We are interested in patterns that are similar to those in the dissolved relationship.

Differences. In addition to the similarities, we are also interested in the differences between the current relationship and the former marriage. In other words, is the couple trying to shape this relationship in ways that are different from the dissolved marriage?

The Wrap-Up

Like the wrap-up following the DRH, the wrap-up of the exploration of previous marriages is designed to indicate to the couple what the counselor perceives in the previous dissolved marriage. This wrap-up, like the wrap-up following the DRH, is not meant to be judgmental but rather descriptive. The idea is to help the couple focus on what is new and different in their current relationship and what is similar and could cause conflict in the new marriage. Thus, in style and shape, this wrap-up is no different from the items discussed in "The Wrap-Up Session" in Chapter Four.

Part 4: FOE

The purpose of Part 4 of the remarital counseling process is to explore the degree of separation between each of the persons and their family of origin. As with a couple preparing for their first marriage, Part 4 is designed to help the couple assess the nature of the parental marriages, whether they have an excessive attachment to their parents, and whether they will be able to take responsibility for their own lives. The issues discussed in Chapter Five regarding parents as models, the format for exploration, the method, the wrap-up, and saying good-bye all apply in the remarital counseling process.

Part 5: Wedding Preparation

This final counseling session consists of an exploration of the mechanics of the wedding and theology, and is designed especially for clergy. This portion of remarriage counseling is identical to Part 5 as discussed in Chapter Five.

Part 6: Postwedding Session (Bonus)

The idea here is to have the couple commit to a counseling session some six months after the wedding. The purpose of the session is to follow up with the couple in a positive form and allow them to seek clarification, obtain further counseling, and provide the counselor with feedback on the counseling given. The counselor can encourage the couple to continue to strengthen their marriage. This was discussed in more detail in Chapter Five.

Remarital Counseling with Stepparents

In an excellent article on spouse and stepparent roles in remarriage, Kay Pasley, David Dollahite, and Marilyn Ihinger-Tallman report that their literature review reveals few differences in marital satisfaction between adults in first marriages and those in remarriages. They say that there appears to be "no support for the seemingly compelling hypothesis that bringing children into a remarriage lowers the odds of marital success." Thus they conclude that "it is not the presence or absence of children per se which affects the spousal relationship. Instead, the dynamics of interaction around child-related issues offer a key for understanding marital outcome and the nature of the spousal relationship."[2]

The approach presented here for doing remarital counseling with stepparents is the model described previously of generally no more than eight counseling sessions to explore and strengthen the couple relationship. Our model does not deal with major problems around stepparenting or parenting issues. If such a need arises, the remarital counselor must select one of several options. He or she could include a more in-depth stepparenting focus along with the remarital counseling process and thereby increase the overall number of counseling sessions. The counselor could continue with the remarital counseling to its conclusion and then do the stepparenting focus, perhaps also including the children in counseling sessions. Yet another option is to refer the couple to another counselor or program such as that offered by local groups of the Stepfamily Association of America, an organization whose mission is to provide education and support to stepfamilies.

Stepparents' Perceptions

An interesting and useful study of married stepparents who participated in family therapy has implications for us in remarital counseling, even though our approach is counseling couples before the wedding.[3] In addition, since some stepparent couples will be cohabiting when we see them in remarital counseling, there may be greater similarities between their concerns as they come to remarital counseling and those in the study who were already married.

The researchers found that the greatest concern that stepfamilies brought to therapy was stepfamily functioning, that is, anxiety or depression about how things were going in the stepfamily. These families also had concerns about the ways in which both the biological and stepchildren's parenting needs were being met. Related concerns involved confusion about stepparents' roles and household rules.

The authors suggest that therapists support stepfamilies by validating and normalizing their feelings and experiences. Helping the clients realize that "their feelings and concerns were 'normal' was a great relief as it restored their feelings of self-esteem."[4] Another implication for remarital counselors is that many of the stepparents' concerns relate to attaining or enhancing communication, conflict-resolution, and decision-making skills. Addressing topics such as finances and the current marital relationship was also helpful to these clients.

Suggestions for Working with Remarital Stepparents

The following specific suggestions are intended to enhance the awareness, sensitivity, and thereby the competence of the remarital counselor. Several of the suggestions are also important for the premarital counselor working with first marriages.

• Keep in mind that the family is an interactional system. The couple is a part of that system. Whenever something affects one family member, it directly and indirectly affects all family members.

- The counselor should help the couple realize that their feelings and experiences as a parent or stepparent joining (and thereby creating) a new family system are normal.
- Both flexibility and closeness are important. The counselor should help the remarital couple focus first on increasing couple flexibility in dealing with day-to-day issues. Closeness will then follow. PREPARE-MC assesses these dimensions.
- The remarital counselor should help the couple build a strong sense of closeness as a basis for effective parenting and stepparenting.
- The counselor should help the couple clarify expectations regarding parenting and stepparenting behaviors and roles.
- Since all members of a stepfamily do not share the same history, counselors should encourage the remarital couple and children to understand each other's pasts as they build the future. Having gone through the DRH with the counselor, the couple can share their own history with the children.
- The remarital counselor should help the couple face the losses and changes in previous family relationships that accompany remarriage and the formation of a new family.
- In remarriages where only one partner has previous parenting experience, the counselor should encourage the couple to participate in parent education or training prior to the wedding.
- The remarital counselor should encourage the couple and children to seek counseling or stepparent educational programs after the wedding.

In this chapter we have provided an overview of the dynamics of remarriage and stepparenting. We have also presented specific methods and approaches for counseling with couples who are in the remarital situation. References were made to earlier parts of the book that also elaborate on methods for counseling with such couples. The next chapter presents a model and considerations for group counseling.

Chapter Eight

| **Group Counseling**

Group premarital and remarital counseling is, by our definition, more a counseling process than a teaching process. In a counseling process, the couples involved have the opportunity to work in a small-group setting and focus on various significant aspects of their relationships. We also differentiate the setting: a small group of couples for counseling and a large group of couples or individuals for education.

Format is another distinguishing characteristic. In a counseling process, in which the couples have a small-group setting, the discussion has structure, but individuals and couples can explore significant issues at an appropriate psychological or emotional level. In the educational approach, with a larger group of persons, the structure generally does not allow as much individual exploration or deviation from the prearranged format.

There are also differences among group guidance, group counseling, and group therapy. Group guidance is basically an educational approach, with the main focus on having participants acquire information and skills. In group guidance, the group leader acts primarily as an instructor or teacher.

In group counseling, the focus is on small-group interaction, which is designed to facilitate self-understanding, increase the participants' awareness of themselves and their partners, and improve interpersonal relationship skills. The leader's primary role is that of a counselor and relationship facilitator.

In group therapy, the purpose is similar to that of counseling, but a greater concern is given to unconscious motivations, emotional problems, and the goal of personality reorganization. The role of the leader is that of a psychotherapist.

The Role of the Counselor

The counselor's role in group premarital and remarital counseling can most appropriately be described as that of a guiding facilitator. Because the process is structured, an element of guidance exists. But because the goal is also to aid individual and relationship development, there is also an element of counseling.

We recommend that the counselor be quite active in the sessions. Primarily, the counselor will introduce topics and concepts that relate to the specific goals of the session. The focus should be on the couple. Therefore, the talk and interaction should be primarily between them and not between them and the counselors or other group members. Although the main focus is on the premarital or remarital couple and their relationship, significant relationships can also exist between the couple and the counselors and between other couples or individuals in the group. Counselors who are aware of this can use the relationships to help couples develop and grow. We think that it is important for counselors to serve as models and to create safe and trusting environments in which the couples can understand each other and grow together. All of this is a way of saying that counselors are models of communication, teaching skills in communication, conflict negotiation, and so forth.

Advantages and Disadvantages of the Group Format

In evaluating the advantages and disadvantages of using the group format in counseling, we want to keep in mind our overall goal of premarital and remarital counseling. That goal is to enhance the relationship so that it might develop into a satisfactory and stable marriage.

Advantages

There are several advantages of group counseling. The counselor must carefully evaluate these advantages in light of the advantages of using the conjoint couple format rather than a group format.

More economical use of counselor time and client money. If the same outcome can be achieved with six couples in a small-group process as with a single couple in a conjoint couple process, obviously it is a more economical use of the counselor's time to use the group format. In regard to client fees, it is often the case that the premarital or remarital couple pays a smaller fee for group counseling than for conjoint counseling.

Influence of peers. In group counseling, peer influence is generally a helpful factor in the process. Our experience in group premarital and remarital counseling is somewhat different in regard to peer influence. That is, while a couple is interested in and influenced by other group members, their highly emotional involvement with each other is such that the influence of peers is significantly less than it would be in other forms of group counseling or at other points in the persons' lives.

The "not alone" feeling. It is a common and positive experience for couples in a group premarital and remarital counseling program to realize that other couples share the questions and adjustments they may be experiencing. Through the group interaction, the couples learn that they are not as unique as they thought. Premarital counseling pioneers Vera and David Mace identified this as the "intermarital taboo." Couples in marriage enrichment groups often find that other couples experience the same kinds of problems and questions. This discovery can significantly reduce whatever anxiety or stress the couple has felt.

Direct education. It is helpful for couples to see how others have worked out similar problems or are presently working them out. It is also easier for a person or couple to see others' problems than it may be to see their own. We like to think of group premarital and remarital counseling as a consciousness-raising experience for the participants, who learn from other couples in the group context.

Satisfaction of helping others. In a group process, all members are in some ways counselors as well as participants; they help one another. This can increase the self-esteem of all group members. We would add that the helpfulness of the group experience can serve as a very important model for continued growth throughout the marital relationship. We suspect that couples who have satisfactorily completed a group premarital counseling experience will be likely to participate in marriage enrichment experiences later in life, with the goal of continuing to help themselves, their relationship, and others.

Reality reflection. Groups have many "mirrors," who provide "reality reflection." This happens when people point out something to a group member and keep the member focused on it, even though he or she is attempting to avoid looking at or dealing with it. We really consider this to be a weak advantage in premarital and remarital counseling groups because the focus in such groups is usually less intensely on the individual group members and more intensely on the couples or the relationships. The reality reflection does operate, however, on a broad level when the couples are concentrating together on issues and when the larger group is concentrating on specific aspects of the group process (the need for affection, role as wife or husband, and so forth).

Disadvantages

Following are several of the disadvantages of group counseling. The counselor has a responsibility to evaluate these disadvantages in light of the desired counseling outcomes.

Spouse inhibition. The possibility exists that either or both of the premarital partners might feel less free to talk in a group because of the presence of other group members.

Problems that are too intimate. Some couples might be reluctant to discuss certain problems, feeling that they are too intimate to be exposed to the entire group. In addition, in group premarital and remarital counseling, where some of the relationships may be relatively new and somewhat insecure, the individuals may have rather strong inhibitions about discussing certain topics or concerns in front of their prospective spouse, not knowing how he or she may react or respond.

Premarital and remarital counselors need to consider all of these factors in deciding whether or not the group setting is appropriate for them and their particular clients. We suggest that in making this decision, counselors list the pros and cons and consider factors in addition to those just discussed.

Design Issues of Group Premarital Counseling

The first consideration for the counselor is whether to have both premarital and remarital couples in the same group. We have found that it is best to offer separate groups for these two types of couples. While there may be exceptions to this, generally the couples are different enough in such things as previous marital experience, age, and parenting or stepparenting concerns, that separate groups are advisable.

Whether the group consists of couples preparing for first marriages or for remarriage, there are a number of design or structural issues to address as the counselor considers the use of the group counseling format. We have found several factors that are of most relevance to premarital and remarital counseling situations.

Pregroup Screening Interview

We believe that it is essential for the counselor to interview each couple before beginning the group process. The primary goal of this interview is to ascertain whether or not the couple is appropriate for and will benefit from group counseling. We have found that the majority of couples seeking premarital and remarital counseling are appropriate for the group process, but there are some who are not. Those who should routinely be screened out are couples who have a primary relationship problem or dysfunction, couples who are for some reason opposed to the group context, and couples who are not committed to the counseling process itself. The reader will see that the underlying concern here is to keep out those couples who are atypical and who would be disruptive to the other couples in the group.

We recommend that the screening interview be conjoint, like the group counseling sessions themselves. Occasionally, because of a specific need that arises with a couple or an individual, we arrange for individual or conjoint sessions outside of the group once the process has begun. However, these are arranged on an ad hoc basis and are not a routine part of the group process.

The screening interview needs to be more than an explanation of what the group counseling process is all about. The counselor needs to ascertain whether the couple will be appropriate for the process. In the majority of cases, the counselor's clinical impression, along with the client's perception of his or her own participation, will be adequate. We do not, therefore, routinely employ a psychological test or screening instrument as part of the screening interview.

Co-counselors

In establishing a premarital or remarital counseling group, the counselor must consider whether or not to use a co-counselor. We believe that a co-counselor is desirable, particularly if the counselors are of opposite sexes. The reason we prefer this model may be obvious. We can not overemphasize the importance and impact of male-female modeling, particularly in the discussions, which are a significant aspect of the counseling process. In the group context, where there will be four to six heterosexual couples, we believe that it is desirable to have a man and a woman as co-counselors.

The co-counselors do not need to be (and usually are not) married to each other. They do, however, need to be well acquainted and to have a positive relationship. As one can imagine, the various content and value considerations in premarital and remarital counseling are a significant part of the process. It is important, therefore, for the co-counselors to have resolved any major differences or questions between themselves on such topics.

Group Size

Although the size of the group can vary, it appears that groups of four to six couples provide the most exciting and productive experiences. Groups that contain fewer than four couples, we find, tend to exhibit less vitality. The smallness of the group tends to eliminate discussion, because the variety of backgrounds necessary to stimulate group discussion is not present. In groups with more than six couples, we find that it is difficult to have enough time to interact with and attend to all the persons involved. We have also found that with more than fourteen people in a group, patterns can develop regarding involvement and withdrawal from the group that are difficult to change. Discussion and interaction by all participants are important aspects of the group process, and these can be eased by the recommended group size. In addition, we have also found that if couples who have committed themselves to the process are selected in the pregroup screening, all six couples (and almost never fewer than five of the six original couples) will complete the counseling process.

Frequency and Length of Sessions

We recommend that each group session last two and a half hours. Articles dealing with group premarital counseling have noted that session length varied from two hours to six hours, with some programs including marathon sessions of eight or more hours. Our goal here is to attempt to structure a meaningful time block that will be repeated weekly for a number of consecutive weeks. We have found that two and a half hours is long enough to accomplish significant amounts of work, yet not so long that it becomes tiring. This consideration is particularly important because counselors frequently will need to conduct the sessions in the evening, after both counselors and couples have had full days.

We believe that the goals of premarital and remarital counseling can be accomplished in five or six consecutive sessions of two or two and a half hours each. We recommend that the sessions be held on a weekly basis. Such a procedure communicates to the participants the time span during which the experience will take place and suggests to them the involvement that will be necessary in order for them to accomplish as much as possible within the relatively short period of time.

Group Composition, Setting, and Environment

One issue that needs to be considered in any group counseling program is whether or not the group is to be open or closed. The open group allows for the addition of couples as the group is in process. In closed groups, only those couples who begin the group with the first session are included. Because of the structured format and the time-limited nature of the premarital and remarital counseling process, we require the group to be closed.

Little needs to be said regarding the group setting other than that the room should be adequate in size, comfortably furnished, lighted, and heated. These are administrative details that the counselors must ensure before the group sessions.

Another environmental consideration that should be discussed with the participants during the pregroup screening interview is appropriate dress and attire. The goal here is to have the participants wear comfortable and nonrestrictive clothing that allows them to move without inhibition, yet is modest and inoffensive to other group members.

Homework and Assessment Inventories

We believe that an important aspect of premarital and remarital counseling is the participants' completion of various types of homework assignments between the group counseling sessions. Homework assignments are vital in translating into reality the experiences that have been generated or discussed in the group setting. We believe that effective exploration and change require application and work, which are the goals of the homework assignments. Counselors must be ready and able to generate specific assignments to assist in the counseling process. Counselors will also need to follow up on the homework assignments routinely at the beginning of the next session in order to tie together in a coherent fashion the counseling process and events transpiring in the lives of the participants.

Also, our group process requires the participants to complete questionnaires or assessment inventories. When using the PREPARE and PREPARE-MC inventories in our premarital or remarital groups, we use exercises in *Building a Strong Marriage Workbook,* which the counselor receives when the inventory report is returned from scoring. These exercises are introduced in the group counseling session, and then completed by the couple as homework assignments.

Confidentiality

Confidentiality is crucial in all counseling, including group counseling. Confidentiality needs to be explained in the precounseling screening interview and reinforced throughout the counseling process. Counselors will need to define and implement their own methods of ensuring confidentiality. For example, whenever assessment devices or questionnaires are used, counselors must ask themselves (and explain to the participants) whether or not the results of the questionnaire or the device are to be shared with the entire group, or between the counselors and each couple, or between the counselors and each individual participant. The guidelines are to focus on and clearly insist on confidentiality. We know of no instances where confidentiality has been violated to the detriment of the group or its participants once the issue has been dealt with and has become an ongoing part of the group process. In fact, confidentiality itself becomes an important aspect of bonding and group cohesiveness.

A Group Premarital and Remarital Procedure

We find that there is an appropriate overlap and redundancy between the goals and processes used in group and in conjoint couple counseling before marriage. Certain aspects of the group approach, therefore, will be familiar from earlier chapters. Similarly, some ideas that are presented in this chapter would work very well in a session in which a counselor is seeing an individual couple.

As previously discussed, there are a number of decisions that counselors must make regarding the structure and format of the premarital counseling sessions. We assume that the following decisions have been made: (1) a man and woman will function as co-counselors; (2) the counselors will hold a screening interview with each couple; (3) five or six couples will have been selected for the group; (4) the group will meet for two-and-a-half-hour sessions during five or six consecutive weeks; (5) the couples in the group will be either first marriages or remarriages, but not both; (6) ideally, all couples will have been in their present relationship for at least three months; (7) all couples will have sought counseling voluntarily to strengthen their current and future relationship.

We have developed the following general outline to serve as an overall guide to co-counselors planning the sessions.

Session 1

In the first session, the initial focus is on the process of getting acquainted. A getting-acquainted procedure involving all group members is essential as part of the first session. Some counselors prefer to have everyone wear name tags with first names. Other counselors use a verbal procedure, asking each individual in the group to introduce himself or herself and to state some significant event or fact that would help the group remember and know the person. We have found this to be useful. In addition, we have found that after names have been given, it is useful for the couples to introduce themselves as couples, stating something of significance about their relationship, past history, or future plans. The goal is not to gain a great deal of information about the individuals and couples, but to give them a chance to talk and become somewhat involved in identifying themselves, their partners, and other group participants.

Following the introductions of couples, the counselors introduce themselves as a counseling team to the group and discuss their professional relationship. The counselors then ask each of the couples to introduce their relationship or their plans for the marriage to the group, explaining briefly where they met, stating interesting and relevant facts related to their courtship to date, and, if applicable, saying what wedding plans or goals they have set for themselves. The counselors then discuss in capsule form an overview of the proposed five-session group counseling format.

After the initial introductions and getting acquainted, the group will undoubtedly be somewhat relaxed. The counselors can then provide additional structure by briefly presenting administrative or procedural issues such as length of meeting time, scheduling of breaks, review of expectations about confidentiality, and related matters.

The next task for the group is to identify the specific goals that each couple wishes to achieve in the premarital or remarital counseling process. The counselors demonstrate a procedure for articulating these goals, involving speaker and listener role-playing. During the remainder of the session, each couple can practice the speaker and listener roles, focusing on the specific goals or outcomes that they hope to accomplish during counseling. The homework assignment is to continue to use the speaker and listener role exercise with nonthreatening topics for thirty minutes daily on five of the upcoming seven days. We may also introduce and practice the white and red bean exercise (discussed in Chapter Nine) instead of or along with the speaker-listener technique.

During the last half hour or so of the session, the counselors administer the PREPARE or PREPARE-MC inventory. This will allow ample time for the inventory to be mailed for scoring, for the results to be returned to the counselors, and for the counselors to study the results in preparation for giving the clients feedback during the third session.

Session 2

In the second group session, the homework assignment follow-up is the first procedure. Counselors discuss and correct any problems that group members have found with the counseling process. Counselors solicit reactions to and information about the process from all group participants. Particular successes with the speaking and listening roles or the white and red bean exercise are also discussed. If it is appropriate, a couple may be asked to role-play or recall one of their homework interactions that was particularly stimulating or helpful.

The primary goal of the second session is to explore the personal history and parental modeling of each of the individuals. In order to assist our work with this process, we draw two lines in the shape of a "Y" on newsprint. We have found it useful to obtain a large piece of newsprint and marking pencils for each couple, leaving tape around the room so that couples can go to the wall and write on the newsprint as they discuss their time line. The counselors begin by drawing a "Y" and explaining that one fork of the "Y" indicates John and the other fork of the "Y" indicates Mary. The intersection of the forks of the "Y," resulting in a single line, is the point at which their relationship began. The counselor then begins by asking Mary (or John) to discuss the significant aspects in her childhood that helped her to evolve to the person that she was when she met John. The events are placed on their separate time lines.

It is assumed that John and Mary volunteered to help the counselors demonstrate this particular aspect of the group process. The counselors may already have obtained some demographic and background information on the couple through a questionnaire or inventory that the couple completed when they applied for group counseling. Throughout the individual life history process, the counselors listen for various influences that parents, schools, jobs, and other dating (or marital) relationships have had upon the individuals.

As discussed in detail in Chapter Five, parents are models for husband-wife interactions. One goal of the premarital counseling process is to help the couple identify the impact that parental modeling has had on them and at the same time to grow and progress beyond the model the parents provided. Growth and development beyond the parental models is necessary and appropriate. Although the model the parents provided may have worked well for them, it is unlikely that by itself it will work for the adult child, who will be joining another person with another history of parental modeling to form a new marital relationship and model. The counselors, then, serve as guiding facilitators, assisting the couple in identifying their parents' models and moving beyond them.

In helping the couple examine the effects of parental modeling, the counselors could explore five areas. We present these areas only as suggestions. Counselors are encouraged to expand or modify these areas as they deem appropriate. We suggest that counselors present and discuss as many areas of parental modeling as there are couples in the group. The procedure, then, is to have each couple discuss one of the areas of parental modeling with the counselors and before the other couples in the group. We would explore with each of five couples one of the following areas.

1. *Demonstrating affection.* The first area deals with the demonstration of affection as modeled by the parents. It is important to explore when, where, and how the couples' parents demonstrated affection. Was affection openly displayed, or were there very few displays of affection? Was touching a natural and frequent occurrence, or was it taboo? Misunderstandings and problems can arise in premarital and marital relationships if the partners have different expectations and interpretations about affectional practices. For example, if Larry is undemonstrative and does not put his arm around Susan, Susan may feel unloved. Conversely, Larry may feel rejected if every time he attempts to hold Susan's hand in public, she feels uncomfortable and rejects the hand-holding, an affectionate move by Larry. As differences in parental modeling and home experiences are discussed and discovered, a notation is made on the time line for the couple to discuss this area further. It is important for couples to resolve their different expectations

for their relationship. (Topics such as affection will be excellent content for the later focus on conflict negotiation and resolution.)

2.   *Companionship and shared activities.* The counselors focus on a new topic with a different couple. The second area of exploration for the individuals relates to companionship and shared activities. Did the parents socialize as a couple, or primarily as individuals? In some families, the husband's primary form of companionship is with other men, in such activities as fishing, hunting, and so on. How about parent-child companionship? Did the parents tend to socialize with the children or without them? Were there sex-linked pairings, such as Dad doing things with the boys (his son or other men) and Mom doing things with the girls (daughters or other women)? What social modeling did the individuals observe in other adult couples? What individual expectations does each have regarding social activities that include or exclude the future mate?

3.   *Money and finances.* Moving on to a different couple, the counselors explore a third area of parental modeling—money and finances. Here we explore not only the standards of living of each parental family, but also the parents' spending habits and methods of handling money. What value did parents place on money and material things? How did they handle money? Who paid the bills? Who managed the money? Was some of the responsibility shared? How did they make decisions about spending money?

4.   *Religion.* The counselors next focus on another couple and move into the area of religion. Religion and values are another area in which parents will have influenced a child. By religion, we do not mean simply the parents' avowed denominational affiliation, but more important, their religious activity and involvement. Did both parents practice religious activity? Did neither parent? Was religion a part of only one parent's life? Based on the parents' influences, what expectations and practices relating to religious habits and customs does the young person currently have and expect in the marital relationship?

5.   *Discipline and children.* Moving on to the last couple (assuming a five-couple group), we consider the modeling of the parental home regarding children and discipline. At some point, the parents began a family. How did the parents handle the children? What did the young person learn about being a parent from being a child in his or her home? Young couples frequently have

many ideas about raising children based on their own experience of being a child and being raised according to certain guidelines and assumptions. Each person's understanding of the meaning of being a child has much to do with the particular parental home in which he or she was raised.

These areas, then, should be explored individually by each group member. As was mentioned previously, the counselors should not only consider the topics that have been suggested. By listening carefully, counselors can discover other topics to pursue. For example, it is not uncommon for topics such as parental use of alcohol and other chemicals or drugs or handling of physical illness to be explored in the same manner as the five suggested areas.

The homework assignment for this second session is for the couples to continue discussing all of the areas. If five couples and five areas were discussed in the group session, each couple would have discussed only one of the topics. During the coming week, the couples can focus on the other four areas. The counselors can offer a very short review of the speaker and listener roles, with the admonition that as couples talk together about the content areas, they should attempt to improve their communication.

Session 3

The counselors begin the third session by eliciting the couples' reactions to the previous week's discussion of the five areas. Any problems or concerns that arise are appropriately discussed with the group.

After this, the counselors shift the focus from the individuals' history to the present premarital relationship. They start by again constructing the time line, beginning at the point at which the couple first met or first noticed one another and continuing up to the present, the base of the "Y." The counselors demonstrate the process by asking one of the couples to serve as a model. The counselors ask, "When did you first meet? How did you first meet? What year was this, and what were you doing? What are your recollections of your first meeting? Who initiated dates or continued the relationship? When did you each become more interested in the other? What attracted you to the other person? As you got to know the other person, what did you like and dislike about him or her? How were the two of you different from each other? How were you similar? How did your level of commitment change over time? What first entered your mind when you thought you might marry this person? When did the two of you initially discuss marriage? When did you tell someone else about your intent to marry? Whom did you tell? How did those who matter to you react to your relationship with this person?" These questions and many others are asked. As this process unfolds, the counselors can make brief notes on the time line indicating important dates and events.

The focus here is on helping the couple further discover and uncover what it is about the relationship that attracts them and has led them to this point. The counselors need to keep in mind that at this time, most of the couples will, in fact, be psychologically married. Each partner has already committed himself or herself to the other person and has no intention of changing or altering that commitment. Sometimes, however, one person in a relationship may not have made a commitment. Occasionally, neither person has really done so. The exploration—discovering the nature of the commitment—is therefore crucial.

At this point in the session, the counselors will take one of three routes. If the couples have taken the PREPARE or PREPARE-MC inventories, the counselors will discuss the concepts and goals of those inventories. The counselors will follow the *Counselor Feedback Guide* for Feedback Session 1, provided in the materials that are part of the PREPARE/ENRICH Program. This includes two couple communication exercises and a ten-step procedure for resolving couple conflict. These then become the bases for homework assignments for the couples.

In another case, the counselors may have chosen FOCCUS as the inventory to administer to the couples. In that case, the counselors would give information about that inventory in an interactive discussion process involving the couples.

A third alternative is to discuss several interpersonal dimensions in premarital and remarital relationships. These interpersonal areas may also be combined in the feedback about the results of the inventories discussed earlier. By now, each couple should know something about their individual developmental histories, should have reviewed the salient dimensions of their own relationship and courtship history to the present time, and should have improved their communication skills. The goal of providing these interpersonal relationship dimensions is to help the couple explore these areas and to discover how they might deal with each other and the suggested content or topics. Thus, the counselors are concerned with both the content focus and the interactional process.

The areas are quite similar to those discussed earlier in this book. We present them here for your continued consideration in the group context.

1.   *Friends and socialization.* Exploration here focuses on the extent to which friends are primarily his, her, or mutual friends. Do the partners see themselves as making new friends as the relationship develops, or are they likely to carry over old friends from the days before their relationship?

2.   *Activities.* What kinds of recreational and nonvocational activities does each of the persons enjoy alone? Together? What are their individual vocational or professional plans and goals? How does the future mate fit into these plans? How does each feel about the other's vocational plans and goals?

3.   *Religion or values.* This area focuses on the meaning of marriage to each partner and explores the psychological, emotional, and legal dimensions of the marital relationship. What religious practice does the couple wish to maintain in their life? What sort of the religious activity does each want to pursue in marriage? How are the partners similar and different in this area?

4.   *Geography.* In this area, counselors ask each participant: "What was your geographical environment as you grew up? For example, was it city, suburb, or country? East Coast, Midwest, or West Coast? Cold climate or warm? Did your geographical experiences coincide or conflict with those of your future spouse? What are your geographical preferences after marriage?"

5.   *Affection and sex.* Assuming that there has been an affectional component in the relationship up to this point, counselors ask whether it has been what each expects and desires. They ask each partner: "How might your upbringing and previous experience influence your demonstration of affection in this relationship? Do you have adequate information about sex? Have you and your future mate discussed male and female physiology and

contraception? What are your expectations about giving and receiving affection in your relationship now? After marriage?"

6. *Budget and finances.* Ask such questions as: "Have you discussed your financial situation? Are the two of you comfortable with it? After marriage, who will handle money? As you begin the marital relationship, who will earn the money? What are your short-term and long-term goals and plans regarding financing and budgeting?"

7. *In-laws and parents.* Questions in this area include: "Did your parents support and encourage your premarital relationship with this person? What expectations do your parents have for you individually? As a couple? How have you reacted to your future in-laws during your premarital relationship? How might this affect your marriage? What are your particular ideas and expectations regarding your future mate's interaction with your parents?"

8. *Roles.* Counselors ask what roles each person expects to fulfill as a husband or wife in the marital relationship, what it means for each to be his or her partner's wife or husband, and how various roles in the relationship will be negotiated and changed.

9. *Physical health.* Questions in this area might be: "Have there been any major illnesses in your personal medical history that might have an impact on your marriage? What is likely to be your reaction and how might you cope with illness in your spouse? Do you have specific activities or plans that you will implement to maintain your physical health? Do these include your spouse?"

10. *Children.* Counselors should ask each person: "What are your individual goals regarding the number and spacing of children? Have you discussed family planning and contraception? If you do have children, what will be your goals as parents? What specific goals will you have for your children?"

At the end of this counseling session, the couples are instructed to discuss two of the ten areas per day and to mention at the next session those areas that were a problem to them and those that were relatively easy to discuss. It might be useful for the counselors to prepare a page summarizing the ten areas and listing sample questions that the couples can use in their dialogue during the week.

Sessions 4 and 5

It should be apparent from the material presented so far that there will undoubtedly be variations in the tempo and fullness with which various groups and counselors deal with the material. Thus, this point might represent the beginning of the fourth, fifth, or even sixth counseling session. For consistency, we will assume that we are beginning the fourth.

This section begins with a follow-up on the homework assignment in which couples discussed the ten interpersonal dimensions presented the week before and/or information from the PREPARE, PREPARE-MC, or FOCCUS inventories. Particular attention is given to each of the couples as they identify briefly those areas that were easy for them to discuss. The counselors then instruct each couple to identify one of the areas that contained some conflict for them as they discussed it. This area then will be the content on which the skill building of conflict negotiation will be based. A volunteer couple is solicited and the counselors coach them and teach a conflict-resolution and negotiation approach.

At least three different couples should have the opportunity to practice the conflict-resolution model during the group session. This allows them to experience the process firsthand and also allows each couple to observe at least two other couples using the skills that they have themselves learned. It is ideal to structure the time and experience so that each of the couples has an opportunity to participate in the learning process. This is a primary reason for keeping the groups relatively small. Each couple will have an opportunity to participate actively in the learning process when no more than five couples are involved.

Another unit for inclusion in this session involves family-of-origin material. The counselors can design a process similar to that used earlier in constructing a genogram. For couples who have taken PREPARE or PREPARE-MC, it is appropriate to have them do the exercise involving the Couple and Family Map.

We also suggest that this is an appropriate time to discuss financial issues and topics. The counselors can present and use the individual and couple net worth statements and budgeting exercises as discussed in Chapter Nine.

Yet another possibility of material in this session or the next involves intimacy and sexuality. The counselors can modify the suggestions discussed in Chapter Ten for use in the group setting.

At the conclusion of this session, the counselors give homework assignments based on the topics and concepts covered. For example, each couple is to practice the conflict-negotiation skills that have been introduced. They are also asked to review their previously learned skills in speaking and listening effectively. As the couples do this, it will be apparent to them that the communication and conflict-resolution skills go hand in hand. It is difficult to negotiate and resolve conflicts without effective communication. They are similarly asked to continue discussions about their families of origin, their genograms, budgeting, or intimacy and sexuality.

Session 5 or 6

In this session, which is usually the final part of the group premarital process, the primary goal is to summarize and synthesize the learning and experimental components of the previous sessions. Earlier sessions have involved skill building in communication and conflict negotiation, as well as specific areas of content and focus. The counselors help the couples review the material they have covered together.

Counselors should be aware of a number of possible alternatives that may be appropriate at termination. First, it is assumed that most couples will have progressed well and will continue their plans for the upcoming wedding and marriage. It is important at this point, we believe, for counselors to discuss with the couples the possibility that they should come back for a few sessions of postmarital counseling after they have been married for six months to a year. The purpose of this postmarital counseling is to assess the current status of their relationship and to strengthen it even further.

The second alternative involves further premarital or remarital counseling. This would be the case if particular difficulties have arisen. It is possible that through the group counseling process, the couple has determined that their commitment to marriage as previously planned has changed and that they wish to continue the counseling process to explore the nature of this change. We recommend that if continued counseling is appropriate, it is most effectively done on an individual conjoint couple basis, rather than in a continued group setting.

A third alternative is to move from a dynamic premarital or remarital counseling format into a format that includes other family members. This alternative—having each couple meet with counselors and with the couple's parents—is being adopted as a routine procedure in some settings. Because of the large size of the group if each of the five couples were to bring their two sets of parents (a total of thirty persons plus the counselors), we recommend that a session for each couple and their parents be conducted apart from the group process.

There may be other alternatives and other types of conclusions that could complement the group counseling sessions. Again, the counselors need to be sensitive, conscientious, and creative in developing specific approaches to closure that will have meaning for and impact on the particular couples in the group. The counselors should plan the termination with the help of the couples.

Session 6 or 7 (Optional)

The clergy, who may be providing premarital or remarital counseling as preparation for the wedding that they will conduct, will likely include a group session dealing with wedding preparation. Even if the clergy counselor is not the person who will perform the wedding, dealing with wedding preparation and expectations in a group session can be of value if the couples are of the same religious denomination, and may be of interest to those of differing denominations or faiths.

In this chapter we have presented the advantages and disadvantages of group premarital and remarital counseling. A process of conducting group counseling was presented so that the counselor can consider the service provided in this approach. The following chapters detail special considerations and topics that may be included in either conjoint couple or group approaches to premarital and remarital counseling.

Chapter Nine

Communication, Values, Decision Making, and Finances

In this chapter, we wish to present premarital and remarital counselors' perceptions of problem areas for many couples. We will also look at some information provided by never-married students and stepparents to see their perspectives on what premarital and remarital counselors might include in counseling. We will conclude the chapter with an overview of several basic exercises for use with couples; the exercises address issues of communication, clarification of values, decision making, and finances.

Counselors' Perspectives on Areas for Discussion

In a recent study, 238 clergy premarital counselors were asked to estimate the percentage of premarital and remarital couples having problems or complaints in twenty-nine possible areas.[1] This was a diverse group of clergy, representing six denominations from forty-four states and every geographical region in the United States. They reported that during the past year they had provided counseling to an average of six first marriage couples and another three couples in which at least one partner had been previously married. They had done premarital or remarital counseling with 94 percent of the couples that they wed. For *first marriages,* they ranked five problem areas as occurring most frequently and estimated the percentage of couples having that problem. As they saw it, those problem areas were:

Problem Areas	*Percentage of Couples with Problem in Area*
1. Communication	63
2. Unrealistic expectations of marriage or spouse	62
3. Money management, finances	60
4. Decision making, problem solving	55
5. Power struggles	51

For *remarriages,* the five problem areas ranked as occurring most frequently and the estimated percentages of remarital couples having that problem were:

Problem Areas	*Percentage of Couples with Problem in Area*
1. Communication	57
2. Children	57
3. Problems related to previous marriages	49
4. Power struggles	48
5. Money management, finances	47

In the same study, these clergy counselors were asked to rate the five most damaging problems to first marriages and remarriages. For *first marriages* these counselors said that the five most damaging problems would be:

1. Communication
2. Money management, finances
3. Unrealistic expectations of marriage or spouse
4. Alcoholism
5. Physical abuse

In regard to *remarriages,* the clergy counselors ranked the five most damaging problems to be:

1. Communication
2. Alcoholism

3. Unrealistic expectations of marriage or spouse
4. Power struggles
5. Physical abuse

This information points to practical implications for the premarital and remarital counselor. As we noted in earlier chapters, much of a couple's experience during courtship focuses on the emotional and psychological nature of the relationship. Although most premarital and remarital couples function well and are psychologically healthy, the implication from the data cited earlier is that significant issues or problem areas can be identified and dealt with in premarital and remarital counseling.

For example, communication skills can be enhanced or taught. Most couples can benefit from practice in expressing thoughts and feelings and listening to their partner. They can sharpen decision-making and conflict-resolution skills. Financial budgeting, marital roles or responsibilities, parenting, and so forth can be the specific subjects used to practice these skills. Through such skill development or review, the couple immediately enhances their relationship and strengthens their foundation for dealing with problems and crises that will inevitably occur later in the relationship.

Never-Married Students' Perspectives

In another study, the researchers presented 185 Midwestern never-married college students with thirteen topics that might be included in a premarital counseling program.[2] First, the researchers asked the students about their interests in premarital preparation and found that the great majority of them (74 percent) were quite interested or extremely interested in the topics presented. Second, the researchers, Benjamin Silliman and Walter Schumm, examined the content of premarital programs. They concluded: "Results suggest that young adults are interested in both interactive skills, such as listening and conflict resolution, and specific issues, such as parenting and money management. . . . Lower rankings for marital roles, sexuality, and stress management may indicate a corresponding lack of awareness of day-to-day issues in married life."[3]

Stepparents' Perspectives

Another study is of relevance to remarital counselors, even though it focused on a sample of already married stepparents who had sought family therapy for stepparent concerns.[4] This study attempted to find out what stepfamily couples who sought therapy identified as primary problems as they initiated therapy. These clinical researchers found that the greatest concerns at the initiation of therapy were stepfamily functioning (depression or anxiety about how things are working in the stepfamily) and parenting or stepparenting concerns (meeting the biological and stepchildren's needs, confusion about the stepparent role, household rules, and discipline).

These findings suggest some practical points for the family therapist to consider when meeting with stepfamilies. We believe that these also apply to remarital couples where children are involved, so we present them in language related to remarital counseling. First, the couple is the core of the family system. Thus, the counseling sessions should initially focus on the couple, even though there are children involved. Second, effective communication skills can be modeled and taught. Third, learning or enhancing communication and negotiation skills can clarify the partners' role expectations, increase their sensitivity to each other's perspectives, and prepare them for the inevitable stress and changes of stepparenting. Fourth, the counselor can provide support and reassurance to the remarital couple by helping them to understand that their feelings and concerns are real and normal.

Developmental Tasks for the Newlywed Couple

The premarital and remarital counselor is a catalyst and facilitator as the couple evaluates their present relationship, enhances that relationship, and looks to the future. This is particularly true when the counselor raises questions or brings up issues that the couple may not have been aware of or had not discussed openly at an earlier time. The counselor will realize that the following ideas related to the developmental tasks associated with a new marriage will apply differently to couples depending on their age, life experience, and prior marital experience.

Tasks for the New Wife

A new wife has internal and external expectations that she must meet. She has an idea of what it is to be a wife in general and how she will function as the spouse in her new marriage. Being the couple's social secretary and planner and taking the lead in homemaking responsibilities frequently seem to be expected of the wife, regardless of whether or not she is employed outside the home. She is also to be an appropriate marital companion, in-law and family member, community citizen, and friend. If children are involved, she is likely expected to be the primary caretaker and nurturer. The new husband also expects her to be his companion, confidant, sex partner, and so forth.

Tasks for the New Husband

The newly married male has all of the expectations thrust on him that are given to an adult male of his age, social status, and new role as a married person. Typically, society expects him to maintain gainful employment and hold up his part of the family financial responsibility. He is also to be an appropriate marital companion, in-law and family member, community citizen, and friend. The new wife also has expectations for him. She assumes that the new husband will be an adequate provider, companion, confidant, decision maker, sex partner, friend, and that he will fulfill numerous similar expectations.

Couple Marital Roles and Expectations

We believe that the premarital counselor needs to raise issues related to marital expectations and roles with the couple. Numerous complementary and conflicting developmental tasks face the newly married couple. As an example, we will look at a rather straightforward situation that many inexperienced premarital counselors might overlook as an issue for couples in modern society. Our experience has shown that the amount of time and attention that the husband gives to his employment and that the wife devotes to household responsibilities, regardless of her employment status, are basic issues that all couples must work out.

For example, the new husband will likely be trying to establish himself in an occupation and the new wife will be working hard to establish the couple's home and manage the household responsibilities, whether or not she is employed outside the home. Here the marital roles can be complementary or conflicting, depending on the couple's expectations and actions. Things will go well and be complementary if the couple has similar expectations and corresponding behaviors. If both share an interest and responsibility in homemaking, there will likely be little conflict related to these issues and behaviors. On the other hand, if expectations and behaviors are discrepant, conflict is likely.

If, for example, the husband or wife is engrossed in professional work and devotes more time and attention to it than his or her spouse expects, a problem can arise. Or if a well-meaning but insensitive husband shows little or no interest or involvement in the household, conflict can arise. This is particularly true in the early months of marriage, as this is when the couple establishes the home and household as physical and psychological entities.

The reader can create similar scenarios based on personal experience and counseling with various couples. The data from the studies cited earlier suggest issues and topics to include in the counseling plan and premarital and remarital counseling process. Similar areas are presented in assessment inventories such as PRE-PARE, PREPARE-MC, and FOCCUS.

Some Counseling Methods for Skill Development

We have found specific exercises useful in working with premarital and remarital couples. The counselor can modify them to fit his or her particular style or to fit the counseling setting. The exercises might also inspire counselors to develop their own exercises.

White and Red Bean Exercise

This is a simple but powerful exercise that we first encountered in William Lederer's book, *Marital Choices*.[5] Its goals are to make the partners more aware of their unconscious behaviors, to help a person minimize the behaviors that his or her partner interprets as negative, and to increase the behaviors that the partner finds positive.

First, the couple is instructed to obtain a handful of dried red beans and white beans. Most have them in their food supply. If not, they can easily and cheaply purchase them at a grocery store. Really, any two colors of beans or any similar items such as game tokens will do. Coins will also work, with pennies as red and silver coins as white, which reflects a monetary value that relates to the point of the exercise.

Each partner is instructed to carry some beans (perhaps ten) of both colors in their pocket so that they can retrieve them easily. The couple receives the following instructions: "During the coming week, whenever your partner does something that you perceive as positive or pleasant, tell him or her so verbally. The visible way that I want you to show your positive reaction is to hand him or her a white bean. When you receive a white bean, say 'Thank you' or give some other verbal acknowledgment. Whenever your partner does something that you perceive as negative or unpleasant, hand him or her a red bean. Immediately, the partner who receives the red bean asks, 'Why the red bean?' The person who gave the red bean courteously and calmly tells what they perceived as negative or unpleasant and thus why the red bean was given. Remember, the important thing here is that one partner *perceived* an action or intent as negative, not whether the other partner *intended* it to be so. Whether the partner receiving the red bean believes he or she deserves the red bean is irrelevant. The red bean receiver says 'Thank you' and there is no further discussion about it."

As the counselor can see, both partners become aware of how their actions are being perceived, as either "white bean positive" or "red bean negative." Instruct the couple that when a bean is received, it is put in another pocket or cup so as not to be mixed in with the beans to be given. Tell the couple to be generous in giving out white beans. Positive feedback, even about little things, is important. For example, Amy hands Al a white bean and says, "I like it when you smile like that." Al responds by taking the white bean and saying, "Thank you." He then puts the bean in his pocket.

The counselor should also tell the couple not to be hesitant in giving red beans. Red beans should be given for small negative things, for these small things tend, over time, to build into big things. The couple should agree on another time to discuss things further that were raised in the white and red bean exercise and not to discuss them when the beans are given.

The couple is instructed to determine a time each day to tally the number of white and red beans exchanged. The counselor could say, "Now I want you to find a time each day during which you can empty your pockets of the beans that you received during the day. Empty the beans that both of you received into a single cup or jar. Yes, both of you put your beans into the same cup. We do not care who received or gave the most beans of either color. What we do care about, and what you will tally, is the total number of white and red beans that you exchanged each day. The total of white and red beans exchanged represents the number of positive and negative exchanges between you as a couple during the day, and that is what we care about. By becoming aware of how your actions are perceived as positive or negative, I hope that you can increase the positivity in your interaction."

The couple then counts the white and red beans. We suggest that the partners make a simple chart showing the tally of white beans and red beans exchanged each day. They could write the days of the week across the top of a page and graph the number of white beans and red beans for each day. That might look something like Table 9.1, where W = white beans and R = red beans.

We have found that the number of beans exchanged during a day varies, depending on time spent together and the couple's setting. That is okay, though, because the goal of the exercise is to increase awareness, and even a few beans exchanged during a day can increase awareness or confirm how the partners are perceiving each other's actions.

Once this exercise has been introduced, the counselor could tell the couple that they can now use the white and red bean terminology as a fun and personal way of communicating. For example, when Al asks Amy how her day has been, if she responds, "It's

Table 9.1. Tally of White and Red Beans for Each Day.

Color of Bean	M	Tu	W	Th	F	Sa	Su
W	15	10	15	15	20	15	20
R	10	15	5	5	15	5	5

been a red bean day," Al will have some useful information to guide his further interaction with Amy. Also, if the couple do not have beans handy when they are together, they can still use the language. Amy says, "Al, here's a red bean." Al responds, "Why the red bean?" to which Amy says, "You just missed the freeway exit to the theater."

The counselor should follow up on the exercise, and have fun doing so, by asking in the next counseling session, "How was your week—more white or red bean?" The counselor can also review the chart that the couple has brought with them.

"I" Statements

Most counselors are familiar with this basic communication technique. Variations of it are part of almost all communication exercises or programs. An "I" statement is a way to communicate feelings clearly and honestly to a person. This is an important technique that can be introduced or reviewed separately with the premarital or remarital couple, or, for example, along with the white and red bean exercise.

The three parts of an "I" statement are to: (1) describe the *behavior* without blaming, (2) state *feelings,* and (3) state what the *consequences* might be. Thus, an appropriate "I" message might be: "When you are late picking me up *(describes the behavior),* I feel anxious *(states the feeling)* because I think that you might have been in an accident *(states the consequence)."*

Origin of Values Exercise

Another exercise that we have found to be helpful in raising developmental and role expectation issues with couples builds on the value clarification work of Sidney B. Simon.[6] The purpose of this exercise is to help the couple see who may have influenced their values and behaviors on a specific issue or topic. When the partners understand more clearly the roots of their values and behaviors, they are in a good position to negotiate and clarify their expectations and behaviors with their future spouses. Also, we have found that after a couple has been through this exercise on one issue or topic, they can readily use it to clarify others as they arise.

We often create a homework assignment to apply the exercise to another issue before the next counseling session.

We begin this exercise with a piece of paper, usually on a clipboard, for each of the partners. At the top of the page we have printed the heading or ask the clients to write: "Who influences my values and how much?" Below that, we write "Issue:" and leave a space so that each can fill in the specific issue that will be the focus.

First, we determine an issue related to a marital role or value by talking with the couple. For our example here, we will use the issue, "Husband's role as breadwinner in the marriage." Each of the partners is instructed to write that issue at the top of the page in the space indicated. See Figure 9.1.

Next, each partner answers the following questions: Who are eight (or six or ten) significant others in your life? What would they expect of you related to a specific issue? Each partner is instructed to identify significant people in their lives in categories such as mother, father, guardian, brother, sister, grandmother, grandfather, aunt, uncle, cousin, best friend, peer leader, religious leader, teacher, neighbor, famous person that they may not actually know, lover, person who dislikes them. As the partners identify specific categories of persons and then name actual persons in each of the categories, the exercise comes alive. We suggest writing the person's name or initials in parentheses after the category on the page to make thoughts about that person more immediate. The partners are instructed to leave the center of the page blank and to write the categories and names of the persons on the top, bottom, and edges of the page.

The partner is next instructed to list three to five values or ideas by which each of these persons would want the partner to live. We say to the couple, "If I were to talk with each of the people that you have identified on your paper, what values or ideas would they have for you related to the issue 'Husband's role as breadwinner in the marriage?' How would they have you live, related to that issue?" Each partner must then complete the page alone without consulting his or her mate. The counselor may be interested in observing their nonverbal behavior during this time.

The example in Figure 9.1 shows a partially completed page from one partner. After both partners have completed their pages,

Figure 9.1. Origin of Values Exercise.

Issue: "Husband's role as breadwinner in the marriage."

Mother (Alice): Husband is the sole support; wife works outside the home only in an emergency.

Best friend (Sam): Wife works to help the couple get established.

Brother (Jack): Husband = $!

Fiance (Amy): Both will work while we finish school; husband is main wage earner; want to be home when kids are young.

Father (Al): Support your wife!

Religious leader (Pastor Jim):

Boss at work (Susan): You two do whatever you think best; I hope you will still work for me.

Grandmother (Anna):

the counselor instructs each person to look at his or her own page and to consider the variety and the similarities or differences among the values and expectations that these significant people have for them. Then, each partner is to circle each item that he or she also accepts and wants for himself or herself.

The clients are instructed to label the blank center of the page "ME" and to draw lines from the accepted values and expectations to the ME area. These lines would then represent many of the person's values and expectations about the husband's role as breadwinner in the marriage.

At this point, we have the couple take a single piece of paper and write "US" at the top center. They also write the statement:

"Some of our values and expectations related to the husband's role as breadwinner in our marriage." As the counselor might expect, this is the interactional part of the exercise. The couple discusses their two pages together. On the new "US" page, they list the items that they want to or will accept as part of their new marital relationship. Once they have begun this process and the counselor has determined that they understand what to do, it can become an exercise to be completed outside the counseling session. If this is done, it should be followed up at the next meeting with the couple.

This exercise creates other useful information for the individual partners and the couple. Specifically, the items listed on each page that were not circled are presumably those values or expectations that the person rejects. Such information may not have been so graphically brought to the person's awareness before. It may be significant for the individuals to be aware of and to discuss as they plan for their marriage. Will each future spouse be supportive on the particular issue? Is it a major or minor issue for the couple to face? The counselor may find an opportunity to help the couple as they anticipate dealing with their families or significant others on this or other values and expectations examined during the exercise.

The Couple's Financial Resources

We are not financial counselors, nor are most persons who do premarital and remarital counseling. However, our years of working with premarital couples and the results of studies such as those cited earlier in the chapter lead us to believe that the counseling process should raise financial questions and increase the couple's financial awareness. Specific financial and budgeting information is available to counselors and couples from a variety of textbooks, as well as self-help budgeting and family financial planning books, most of which can be found in bookstores and libraries.

At a minimum, it would seem useful for the premarital counselor to provide a simple net worth statement for the couple to fill out. After completing the net worth statement, the couple could fill out a budget worksheet as shown below. A budget worksheet and suggested exercise are also found in *Building a Strong Marriage Workbook*, which is provided to the couple as part of the PREPARE or

PREPARE-MC programs. The couple can use the information from these financial exercises outside the counseling process or within that process, as they learn and practice communication and decision-making skills.

In the net worth statement, the partners list assets at their current market value (what each could be sold for today) and list liabilities (values currently owed to creditors). The net worth is the dollar amount obtained when total liabilities are subtracted from total assets. A sample net worth statement appears in Exhibit 9.1. We suggest that each partner complete his or her own net worth statement that describes his or her current status. The counselor should encourage each partner to list small but important items in all areas. For example, in personal property, they should not forget things such as furniture, kitchen items, tools, and recreational and sports equipment. After each partner has completed a personal statement, the couple can compare and discuss the statements and create one that reflects the information for them as a couple.

Often, this simple exercise reveals information that was not previously known to the other. This is particularly true for remarital couples. An exercise frequently introduces an awareness and bonding that were not previously present in the relationship.

A related but different idea to introduce to the couple is to have them look ahead to the issue of finances after their wedding. The net worth statement describes the assets and liabilities entering the marriage. How do they anticipate using these resources and maintaining or expanding them? That raises the issues of budgeting and the short-term and long-term financial goals for the marriage. The counselor can ask the couple to discuss, agree on, and write down several short-term and long-term financial goals.

Couples often find it useful to project a budget or cash flow statement for their marriage. Looking to the time when they will be married, the couple should project income from wages, interest, dividends, and other sources, as well as expenditures on items such as food, shelter, insurance, recreation, personal items, transportation, and loans. Again, our goal is to have the couple begin or continue a process of gaining information about their material resources so that they can maximize them after the wedding. When a couple enters marriage without both partners' having full knowl-

Exhibit 9.1. Net Worth Statement.

Name of individual or couple:_____

Assets:

Cash $_____

Checking accounts $_____

Investments $_____

Personal property $_____

Home $_____

Automobile $_____

Business $_____

Other $_____

Total Assets $_____

Liabilities:

Rent (past due) $_____

Utilities (past due) $_____

Charge accounts $_____

Credit cards $_____

Taxes $_____

Loan balances $_____

Auto loan $_____

Mortgage $_____

Other $_____

Total Liabilities $_____

Net Worth = Total Assets – Total Liabilities = $_____

edge of their joint financial assets and liabilities, problems related to expectations and trust often develop and have a major negative impact on the relationship.

An often used homework assignment is for the counselor to have the couple project a budget for the first six months or year of their marriage. An outline such as that in Exhibit 9.2 can be used for a basic budget outline.

Exhibit 9.2.   Marital Budget Worksheet.

Combined Monthly Income:

Salaries	$_____
Other	$_____
Total Income	$_____

Monthly Expenses:

Fixed Expenses:		*Variable Expenses:*	
Rent/Mortgage	$_____	Savings	$_____
Telephone	$_____	Contributions	$_____
Utilities	$_____	Food (home)	$_____
Auto loan	$_____	Eat out	$_____
Credit cards	$_____	Clothing	$_____
Auto insurance	$_____	Entertainment	$_____
Health insurance	$_____	Personal	$_____
Other	$_____	Auto	$_____
Laundry	$_____		
Child support	$_____		
Vacation/travel	$_____		
Other	$_____		
Total Fixed Expenses	$_____	Total Variable Expenses	$_____

Total Fixed Expenses $_____ +
Total Variable Expenses $_____ = Total Expenses $_____

Total Income – Total Expenses = Joint Net Worth $_____

Decision Making

As we discussed earlier when we presented the DRH, the counselor should be interested in how the couple has made decisions throughout their relationship. Patterns in decision making are important for the couple to understand and can be the bases for strengths and weaknesses in the marriage. Here, we wish to consider a different approach to understanding the couple's decision making than we presented in the DRH. We now explore an emphasis on expectations and the future, rather than on the past.

We are interested in the couple's expectations as to who will make various types of decisions in the marriage. The goal is developing a clear understanding of what is equitable for both partners. The equity of the decisions and the decision-making process is an important issue for the couple to work out. An appropriate function of premarital and remarital counseling is to provide the couple with a framework for understanding and communicating decision making. Richard Stuart's work with marital couples has provided us with a model that we have adapted for premarital and remarital couples.[7]

The core question is, "Who will make the various kinds of decisions in this marriage?" Many decisions, large and small, face the couple daily. How decisions are made will either build or break the marriage. Following Stuart's model, there are five categories of decision making: (1) wife only decides = W, (2) wife decides after consulting husband = Wh, (3) wife and husband decide together = WH, (4) husband decides after consulting wife = Hw, and (5) husband only decides = H.

We begin this exercise by working with the couple to list on paper or the chalkboard a few decisions that they have made related to their marriage. Deciding when to marry, whether to have an engagement ring, what type of a ring to have, how much time to spend together, and what activities to participate in together are sample items. We then change the focus and present decisions that they are likely to face when married. Such items as what employment the husband or wife takes, where the couple lives, how household responsibilities will be divided, whether or not to have children, when to have children, how to spend leisure time, how much money to donate to churches or charities, how much time is spent in community service, and how to spend vacation time are examples. By this time, the couple can generate further items in the list and we have them brainstorm additional items, leaving space on the page or chalkboard to add items. A partial listing, with space left on the right column for ratings, might look like the one in Table 9.2.

If each partner copies the item numbers, he or she can quickly generate a separate list for individual use. Each person can then rate each item on his or her page by placing a check under the category (W, Wh, WH, Hw, H) based on his or her perception of who should or will make such decisions in the couple's marriage. As they compare and discuss their ratings, the partners clarify expectations.

Table 9.2. Couple Decision Making.

	W	Wh	WH	Hw	H
Before marriage					
1. When to get married			x		
2. How much time to spend together now				x	
3. Whether to have an engagement ring	x				
After marriage					
4. When to have children			x		
5. How household responsibilities should be divided				x	
6. What job husband should take				x	
7. When to get pregnant				x	
8. Number of children to have					x

Opportunities for compromise and adaptability may also arise. Thus, the couple now has a model for clarifying decision making, one that can serve them throughout their marriage. In a troubled or dysfunctional relationship, the counselor would need to spend additional time developing basic decision-making skills or make a referral for more intensive therapy.

Many premarital and remarital couples may have the expectation that the "ideal" is to operate out of the category WH, in which the wife and husband decide together. Not necessarily so! It is likely that the wife and husband have differing areas of expertise and interest. To believe and require that both spouses decide together on all things soon becomes an impossibility and overloads the couple and therefore the marital relationship. In terms introduced in the Couple and Family Map from the PREPARE or PREPARE-MC inventories, the couple would be "overly connected" and have too much togetherness or closeness. The premarital or remarital counselor will serve the couple well by addressing this expectation and discussing its absurdity.

The premarital or remarital counselor should be quite knowledgeable about teaching communication skills. Specific areas such as effective listening and speaking, problem solving, and handling conflict are all important. There are many good books that the counselor could have couples read and apply to their relationship. One such program is Howard Markman, Scott Stanley, and Susan Blumberg's PREP, or Prevention and Relationship Enhancement Program. This program is presented in the book *Fighting for Your Marriage: Positive Steps for Preventing Divorce and Preserving a Lasting Love,*[8] which we recommend.

In this chapter we have presented research results from counselors and clients on their perceptions of topics that should be considered for inclusion in premarital and remarital counseling. Specific exercises and interventions on the topics of communication, values, decision making, and finances were presented and discussed so that the counselor might adapt them for use.

Chapter Ten

Intimacy and Sexuality

We believe that it is important for the premarital and remarital counselor to include information on sexuality for several reasons. First, most couples expect the topic to be addressed in some form and in some depth. Second, although the average marrying age has increased to the mid to late twenties, there are still numerous couples who are not sexually active or educated because of their beliefs and values, and many individuals do marry at a younger than average age. Third, regardless of the marrying age and premarital sexual activity and experience, many people are not well informed about sexual matters, and few have sensitively gone over this information together as a couple.

The EXPLISSIT Model

We wish to present a model that can be useful to the premarital and remarital counselor in conceptualizing the different levels of education or counseling that may be required in helping couples deal with topics and issues such as sexuality and intimacy. The model can also be applied to other topics in family therapy.[1] This model was originally developed to describe four different levels of intervention in sex therapy, but we have found that it directly applies to the counselor working with premarital and remarital couples.

As applied to sex therapy, the four levels of expertise and intervention conceptualized in the original model are represented in the word PLISSIT or P-LI-SS-IT. "P" represents the "Permission" level and consists of the counselor's simply feeling comfortable enough to convey a sense of permission to clients so that they feel free to bring up sexual matters. The next level, which often blends with permission, is providing "LI," or "Limited Information." Many couples and individuals can be helped if the counselor merely provides some basic information, such as an overview of the sexual response cycle. The third level of intervention involves "SS," or "Specific Suggestions," which can be viewed as the sex counseling level. Here, the counselor can offer suggestions to deal with specific sexual problems, or can introduce exercises such as sensate focus to create sensitive understanding and communication. The fourth and most complex level of intervention is "IT," or "Intensive Therapy." This refers to sex therapy.

While we have found that the PLISSIT framework does guide the levels of intervention, we feel that there is an important ingredient missing. That is, simply put, clients and counselors may have certain expectations about counseling, which the model does not include. All clients have some sort of expectation or idea about counseling as a process, and likely some expectation about the premarital and remarital counselor as a person. Counselors' expectations guide their design and delivery of the premarital and remarital counseling process. Thus, we add "EXpectations" to PLISSIT, making the model become EXPLISSIT.

In looking at the EXPLISSIT model for conceptualizing, designing, and delivering counseling, we first examine the possible expectations of both the client and the counselor. What does the client expect about the counseling process? Why are the clients in counseling? What might indicate to clients that premarital or remarital counseling is and has been successful? What does the counselor expect, particularly with this client? What does the counselor expect about outcome?

As an example of the EXPLISSIT model, we look at Mike and Mindy, who present themselves for premarital counseling. The counseling setting greatly influences expectations, so we will define the setting as a church-related counseling center. The counselor, an ordained minister, will be performing the wedding for the couple. The clients might expect (EX) that he will bring up the topic of sexuality, but not discuss it in much detail. The counselor, on the other hand, believes that sexuality is an important part of the sacred concept and practical process of marriage and therefore plans to discuss the topic in some detail with Mindy and Mike.

At the permission (P) level, the counselor may need to reassure the couple that the topic of sexuality is appropriate to discuss and deal with openly. There will likely be some clarification of Mike's and Mindy's comfort with the topic, both in growing up and in their current relationship. The counselor will give them direct and indirect permission to discuss the topic. He will convey this permission through the manner of discussion, the language he uses, and his apparent comfort in discussing the topic.

As he expands the discussion of sexuality to include intimacy and the giving and receiving of affection, he and the couple enter the third level, that of limited information (LI). This limited information might clarify the couple's knowledge, ideas, and definitions about (1) sexuality; (2) intimacy (including social, emotional, cognitive, spiritual, and sexual intimacy); (3) nurturance; and (4) love. The counselor can introduce information appropriate to the setting and purpose of counseling, including, for example, professional or religious information.

The next level, that of specific suggestions (SS), might be termed the sexuality counseling level. Here, the counselor will give Mindy and Mike suggestions or alternatives as they address topics such as sexuality, intimacy, love, and nurturance in their premarital relationship. The key here is what the couple needs or requests. The suggestions could cover almost any issue. For example, the counselor might address ways for the couple to maintain their chastity before the wedding or to overcome previous unhealthy sexual behaviors in the relationship.

We are reminded here of a guideline for sex therapists that directly applies to and is crucial for the premarital and remarital counselor: the counselor should never suggest or do anything that conflicts with the clients' values. The counselor must be sensitive to and not assume knowledge of those values, particularly in the area of sexuality. Thus, the counselor must listen and seek to clarify, and not lead or impose values or points of view.

The last level is that of intensive therapy (IT). This would include dealing with individuals' or couples' sexual problems or dysfunctions. Most premarital and remarital counselors are not trained in sex therapy and therefore cannot deal with such problems. Also, such therapy is beyond the goals and processes of premarital or remarital counseling. In such cases, which are unusual, the individual or couple should be referred to a sex therapist. Premarital or remarital counseling may continue concurrently with the other therapy, or it may be discontinued until the other problems are resolved.

As we present additional material in this chapter, the reader is encouraged to apply the EXPLISSIT model.

Contexts for Counseling Couples About Sex

The issue of whether, when, and what sexual information to include in the premarital and remarital counseling process depends greatly on the nature of the counseling setting. Parish ministers face different issues than do counselors in clinics and agency settings.

Parish Setting

As mentioned previously, a significant proportion of first marriages are performed in the local church. With this in mind, we shall explore a variety of expectations related to sex education and counseling in that setting.

Denominational Expectations

Denominations have a variety of opinions and attitudes toward appropriate sexual behavior and explicit sex education. They also have a diversity of opinions and traditions regarding the role of the pastor as a sex educator. In a general sense, the major denominations, especially the Protestant ones, have officially acknowledged the importance of sexual expression in marriage, perceive sexuality as a gift of God, and encourage positive and wholesome attitudes toward appropriate sexual expression and behavior. In addition, most of the major Protestant denominations have developed curricula for teaching sex education to grade school and high school students and to adults. Thus, on an official and national level, the major denominations support sex education, especially in the context of prewedding counseling. In fact, most of the denominations' official handbooks for marriage preparation include material on sexuality and direct the pastor to discuss this with couples. In broad terms, then, it can be said that governing church bodies encourage and support sex education, particularly in the context of pastoral prewedding counseling.

Nonetheless, there are always specific congregations within a major denomination that may be reluctant or adamantly opposed to including sexual material in a premarital counseling setting. Pastors of the more conservative and evangelical denominations may find explicit support of sex education lacking in their denominational statements and social creeds.

Congregational Expectations

Just as denominational expectations in regard to sex education vary, so do local congregations' levels of comfort with sex education. In some local churches, sex education as part of premarital counseling has a long-established tradition begun by earlier pastors. In other local churches, prewedding counseling is either brief and superficial, or hardly established at all. In these congregations, sex education as part of premarital counseling might be met with great resistance. The pastor ought to research the local attitude in regard to sex education. When parishioners do not perceive the pastor as a knowledgeable or appropriate teacher for sex education, the pastor might consider using a nonclergy professional for the sex education portion. A nurse, physician, or professional counselor could appropriately provide that material to couples.

Couples' Expectations

Couples approaching the premarital or remarital counseling session do so with various expectations in regard to its sexual content. Individuals who have been active in their own denomination and congregation, and who come from religious settings that encourage sex education, will probably expect the pastor to address sexual issues during premarital and remarital counseling. Couples from denominational and congregational experiences that were more negative about sexuality may not expect the pastor to deal with sex education and may be surprised or even angered if such content is introduced. To some extent, therefore, the pastor must evaluate each couple before pursuing sex education with them.

Clinics and Agencies

Social service agencies and counseling clinics are more ambiguous about the role of sex education in their premarital and remarital counseling. Nonetheless, counseling agencies and clinics have implicit expectations regarding the roles of the counselor and the program in helping couples adjust to sexuality adequately.

For physicians in medical clinics conducting prewedding medical examinations, the theoretical expectations are rather specific. The physician's responsibility is to provide both sexual information and birth control information.

We believe couples coming to counseling centers and social service agencies for prewedding counseling also have expectations. They anticipate that the counselor will somehow discuss their sexual relationship. This attitude is supported by the fact that so much appears today in popular literature and in the news media about the importance of a good sexual relationship in maintaining a satisfying marriage.

Sexual Content for Premarital and Remarital Counseling

For premarital and remarital counselors who wish to include a unit on sex education, we have identified three major topical areas that the counselor should include in order to provide relatively complete sexual information.

Biology and Anatomy

Information related to anatomy and the biological functioning of the human sexual system must appear in a sexual unit. This material should include such areas as sexual anatomy and physiology of the male and female, including anatomical structure and function. The counselor is not only presenting information here, but uses correct medical terminology, thereby modeling clear, direct communication about sexuality. For example, the counselor might say to the couple, "It is more accurate to say, 'Having sexual intercourse' than to say 'Having sex.' There are many ways other than sexual intercourse that couples can relate sexually and intimately."

Many excellent books are available to counselors who wish to expand or refresh their sexual information. These are available at secular and religious bookstores or in libraries. Counselors should ask any clerk or librarian to direct them to *Books in Print*. We suggest that the counselor talk with a college or university instructor who teaches a course on human sexuality and perhaps, as a resource, purchase the textbook used in such a course. Also, many of the books used in courses on marriage and the family have excellent chapters dealing with basic anatomy, sexual response, and sexuality.

Sexual Response Cycle and Interaction

The second portion of this unit should include material related to the sexual response cycle and sexual interaction. The counselor can present the four-phase sexual response model of excitement, plateau, orgasm, and resolution. We suggest that the counselor assemble charts or drawings from the aforementioned books and use them when presenting this information. By selecting and compiling such information, the counselor can use material that is consistent with his or her own goals and values and with the context of the counseling.

In addition to the sexual response cycle itself, we find it useful to discuss the differences between the *biological process* of the four-phase sexual response and the *psychological process* of sexual arousal or desire. Couples need to understand the sensitive relationship between the two so that they can avoid misunderstandings.

Family Planning

The counselor should discuss with the couple basic information on family planning and contraception. Here, the counselor again facilitates discussion of the topic, and is not necessarily, or usually, the expert. The discussion for both premarital and remarital couples should include whether they plan to have children, when to have them, the ideal spacing, and the number of children desired. Depending on each partner's family of origin and other personal background and life experience, the partners may have similar or very different expectations in this area. Information from PREPARE or FOCCUS inventories can be included here.

At this point, the counselor should also raise the related topic of expectations for rearing and disciplining children. This is particularly true for remarital couples for whom stepparenting is an issue.

༄༅

In premarital and remarital counseling, topics related to sexuality are not designed to be sex therapy. Rather, this aspect of counseling is sex education and is designed to provide pertinent sexual information. The task is that of helping the couple engage in fulfilling and socially responsible sexual behavior. All premarital counseling providers, whether they be clergy, counselors, or physicians, are expected to have accurate information in the area and (from the clients' point of view) to be able to deal with or respond to almost all concerns and problems that the couple brings them. Regardless of discipline, the counselor needs to be well informed about sexual matters. The counselor must also be sensitive to clients' values.

We believe that all adults should understand pertinent information about sexuality, such as anatomy and physiology, the sexual response cycle, fertility, contraception, and family planning. This is not privileged information for counselors. Premarital and remarital counseling can provide couples with this information and can give them a place to discuss and clarify their values. Counseling assessment inventories such as PREPARE, PREPARE-MC, and FOCUS, which we discussed in Chapter Six, also provide a stimulus for such discussion and clarification.

Chapter Eleven

Special Situations
Very Young and Older First Marriages, Forced Marriages, Conflicted Relationships

The intent of this chapter is to discuss the dynamics and process information that is available about the very young couple, older first marriages, forced marriages, and conflicted couples. A discussion of topics of this nature is, of course, severely limited because statements and conclusions are only generalizations based on large samples of persons. Premarital and remarital counselors must be aware that the individuals or couples in a counseling situation may or may not be similar to the larger group on which the generalizations have been based. Thus it is the counselor's responsibility to apply the information in this chapter carefully in understanding and working with each couple.

As discussed earlier in the book, there is a fairly large body of literature, generated primarily from marital and family sociology, that points to a number of trends and generalized conclusions with which the counselor should be familiar. In many instances, the premarital counselor may want to share with the couple some of the information about the prognosis of marital satisfaction and stability as a part of the premarital and remarital counseling process. In other instances, when specific factors pointing to an unsatisfactory or unstable marriage are uncovered as a part of the premarital or remarital counseling, the counselor may appropriately refer the couple to another counselor or marital therapist who has more specific training for the kind of therapeutic, long-term counseling that may be indicated.

Predictors of Marital Problems

In addition to the topics related to marital quality and success discussed in Chapter One, we will now discuss some predictors of marital problems.

The Younger and Older Premarital Couple

There appears to be great consensus among family sociologists that one of the most reliable predictors of marital stability and success is the age of the partners at the time of marriage. Generally speaking, the younger the couples are at marriage, the more likely they are to divorce. The divorce rate is highest among those who marry before their late teens or early twenties. Data have shown that for men who marry under age twenty, the expected divorce rate is two to three times higher than for those who marry at age twenty-one and older. For females, the data show that women marrying under age seventeen have a divorce rate two to three times that of women marrying after age eighteen.[1]

Information also indicates that the couple, particularly women, entering a first marriage after the age of thirty tend to have less stable marriages than those who marry in their twenties. "Older brides apparently are more independent and more willing to terminate a bad marriage than is true of those who marry in their twenties."[2]

Although this generalization is based on large national samples, the premarital and remarital counselor must be aware that such averages may not apply to the specific couple in counseling. There are also differences in groups and group characteristics that underline the counselor's need to know the clients well. For example, Albrecht, Bahr, and Goodman, cited earlier, found that for a sample of older-than-average marrying couples from Western states, education level seemed to counteract marital instability. They found that couples with college degrees were likely to delay marriage until a later age and had the most stable marriages.

A logical question is, Why is the age at marriage such a determining factor in marital happiness and stability? The answer is not clear. It appears that the older a person is at marriage, the greater the likelihood is that he or she will be emotionally and psychologically mature. Such a person is more likely to have completed schooling and to be in a stable financial situation. Also, those who are older will more likely have prepared for marriage by clarifying their values and life goals and working out good relationships with parents and future in-laws. Yet with the older person it is possible that the individually focused style of living as a single person, as well as personal habits and preferences, can cause difficulty in marital adjustment.

The premarital and remarital counselor may be interested in determining what age is "old enough" for marriage. Fortunately or unfortunately, depending on one's point of view, there is no specific answer to such a question. The data indicate that men below twenty years of age and women below eighteen years of age who marry are at high risk for divorce. Research has indicated that women who married at age twenty-five and men who married at age twenty-eight reported greater marital satisfaction and showed greater marital stability (lower divorce rates) than those who married earlier.

Level of Education

A second major factor that can be significantly related to marital happiness and stability is the amount of education each partner has and whether or not that partner's mate has more education. Studies indicate that those men who complete college have lower divorce rates than those who complete only high school or who leave college without graduating. The trend is for college-educated women to be more satisfied with their marriages than non–college educated women. Also, it appears that more highly educated women are more satisfied with affection in their marriages and tend to be more sexually responsive to their spouses. An apparent caution, however, emerges in relation to education: when a wife has achieved a higher level of education than her husband, there is a greater risk of divorce than if the husband has obtained more education than the wife.

The primary reason for the positive correlation between higher education and marital satisfaction appears to be that the greater education level is associated with a higher income level and economic potential. It is likely, therefore, that income level is a significant variable in marital stability and happiness. This is demonstrated by the finding that well-educated men with low incomes are more likely to divorce than men with less education and a higher income.

Situational Reasons to Prolong a Courtship

David Knox, a marriage counselor, has appropriately summarized four crucial points that, if present in a premarital relationship, may well warrant an extension of the courtship or engagement period.[3] Knox suggests that when the factors are present in any combination or process, the couple should be encouraged to extend the courtship.

The first indication is a short courtship. At least a one-year courtship seems to be an ideal length before marriage. The longer the couple has been involved before marriage, the better will be their opportunity to get to know and observe each other in a wide variety of settings. Thus, a longer courtship decreases the possibility of premarital deception and increases the possibility of a true knowledge and understanding of the other person. This would seem to hold true for persons entering first marriages as well as re-marriages.

The second indication is a lack of money or a poor financial condition at the time of marriage. As we indicated previously, there is a significant positive correlation between the husband's income level and the chance that a couple will stay married. This is not to say that a couple cannot live on a shoestring for a while. However, a poor financial condition apparently must be temporary for a couple to achieve satisfaction and stability in marriage.

The third factor Knox identified is that of parental disapproval. If parents disapprove of or have reservations about a potential mate, the most appropriate action is for the adult child to try evaluating the parental objections objectively. Often, parental concerns and predictions of marital failure are based on their own experience as adult observers of marriages and on what might be termed an intimate knowledge of their offspring.

The fourth reason for prolonging an engagement or courtship is often viewed as a motivation to marry immediately: the condition of premarital pregnancy. However, statisticians and clinicians document that if the woman is already pregnant and the couple marries and keeps the baby, that factor alone greatly increases the likelihood of marital unhappiness and divorce. This outcome is related to the likelihood that all three of the preceding reasons for extending the courtship—short courtship, poor finances, and parental disapproval—exist in this situation.

The Forced Marriage

As we have noted, it is difficult to establish exactly what age is "too young" in regard to marriage. Similarly, it is difficult to establish exactly when a forced marriage or forced premarital situation is occurring. For example, until recent times, it was widely accepted that a wedding was the answer to a premarital pregnancy, which led to a forced or hurried marriage. Similarly, a person living in our society is often expected to be married by a certain age. When they reach the age by which they "should" be married, some people may enter into less than ideal marriages. In considering the issue of forced marriage, therefore, we will regard any marriage as forced when either or both of the partners feel coerced into that particular marital relationship.

Earlier chapters in this book, which focused on the various factors relating to the premarital period and the technique of the DRH, discussed in detail the personal and interpersonal dynamics of the courtship period. As a way of addressing the topic of the forced marriage and in an attempt to refrain from repeating some of the earlier discussions, we will briefly address three positive ways in which a couple can use the courtship and engagement period to strengthen their relationship.

Strengthening Courtship or Engagement

Taking a DRH, discussed in Chapter Four, is an important and effective way to help the couple examine their relationship. An important part of the DRH is the discussion between counseling sessions, in which the couple continues to examine and explore their relationship regarding specific topics and interpersonal areas. If, during the DRH, the counselor finds that the partners do not know one another well, then the counselor should recommend expanding counseling or the engagement period. In that way, the couple can continue their examination of their relationship, focusing on getting to know each other.

A second appropriate use of the engagement or courtship period and the DRH in counseling is for couples to recognize danger signals that can predict marital problems. Knox identifies two danger signals—the on-and-off engagement and frequent and intense arguments. An on-and-off engagement predicts a marital relationship with a similar pattern. The same is true of arguments. In a premarital or remarital relationship, an argument is a quarrel and often does not last long or become permanent. When a couple is married, an argument becomes a fight; it often builds up until frustration, dissatisfaction, or inability to cope with or change the situation leads to divorce. We believe that conflict is unavoidable in premarital and marital relationships. A portion of the premarital or remarital counseling process therefore focuses on anger and disagreements in order to develop the couple's skills in resolving conflict.

Third, we suggest that the engagement or courtship period and the FOE in counseling be used to increase interaction with future in-laws. Significant interaction with parents includes visits to allow the potential spouse to observe firsthand the interpersonal relationships in the family, as well as other factors, such as the family's lifestyle and living habits. Of course, it is possible for a person to be quite different from his or her parents. However, the likelihood is that there are many similarities between the prospective spouse and his or her parents. A very appropriate capstone to the premarital counseling process is to include the parents in a final counseling session, as was discussed in Chapter Five.

Relationship Comfort Level

Research has indicated that it is useful for premarital and remarital couples to assess their relationship comfort level, which is an indication of how each partner feels in relation to the other person. In forced marriages the following six variables that reflect relationship comfort level are often lacking from the relationship:

- Empathy, or the ability to put oneself in the emotional place of the other and to see things freely from the other person's point of view
- Spontaneity, or the open and unguarded expression of feelings
- Trust, or the ability and willingness to be honest and unafraid in the dyadic relationship
- Care, or the ability to have a genuine interest in and concern for the other person
- Respect, or the ability to have a regard for the other person's uniqueness and individuality

The Seriously Conflicted Couple

As pointed out previously in this book, the typical couple who seeks premarital or remarital counseling does so with the idea that the counseling process will encourage and reinforce the upcoming marriage. However, there are couples who show up in the counseling office because of a serious conflict or dysfunction in the premarital relationship. Often such a couple has been referred to the counselor by a friend, parent, pastor, or physician who may have been sensitive to or discovered the conflict or dysfunction during contact with the couple. However, we are also finding that an increasing number of couples seek premarital and remarital counseling on their own when such a concern or problem is present. Perhaps this reflects the decrease in the stigma attached to counseling and therapy, or perhaps it reflects a greater concern for having the marriage be successful and satisfactory. Whatever the reason, the premarital and remarital counselor will need to be alert to the seriously conflicted or dysfunctional couple.

Identifying the Seriously Conflicted Couple

A first clue to the counselor that the client couple has serious conflicts might come during the opening moments of the first session as the counselor listens to the couple state why they are seeking counseling. If the couple says directly that conflict is an issue or problem or they are concerned that it may become a problem for them, the counselor should ask specific questions about the conflict. For example: "How would each of you describe the conflict? What seems to set off the conflict? What happens when the conflict occurs? Does one partner withdraw verbally or physically, do you both battle each other verbally, or is there some other pattern or behavior? Does your conflict ever lead to physical violence? How have you overcome or made up after conflict has occurred?"

Another time the conflict may become apparent to the counselor is during the DRH, as discussed in Chapter Four. As the counselor goes through the relationship history, he or she should be sensitive to many dynamics, including how the couple has previously dealt with differences or conflict in their relationship. The reader will recall that the technique of the DRH is for the counselor to look for and be sensitive to patterns of interaction in the couple's relationship. Therefore, as the couple describes and discusses their relationship history, a pattern of conflict or frustration may become apparent. The counselor notes that pattern across the relationship's time line. Then, at the conclusion of the DRH, as the counselor summarizes with the couple their dynamics, strengths, and areas of concern, a pattern of conflict can be hypothesized or noted and discussed.

Assessment inventories such as FOCCUS and PREPARE are another useful method to indicate possible couple or relationship conflict. The counselor who is trained in the use and interpretation of these inventories will find them very effective in identifying conflict areas, in understanding something about the nature of that conflict, and in deciding how, or whether, to treat the conflict in counseling. For example, the PREPARE and PREPARE-MC inventories identify and report scores on fourteen marital content areas that can be conceptually divided into four groups of common conflict issues:[4]

• *Personality issues.* Four personality characteristics are identified and scores reported in the new (1996) version of the inventories. These are: (1) "Assertiveness—a person's ability to express their feelings to their partner and be able to ask for what they would like"; (2) "Self Confidence—focuses on how good a person feels about himself/herself and their ability to control things in their life"; (3) "Avoidance—a person's tendency to minimize issues and reluctance to deal with issues directly";

(4) "Partner Dominance—focuses on how much a person feels their partner tries to control them and dominate their life."

• *Intrapersonal issues.* Five content areas are identified as intrapersonal: Idealistic Distortion, Marriage Expectations/Satisfaction, Personality Issues, Leisure Activities, and Spiritual Beliefs. These are important because "Couples must often contend with individual differences in personality, interests, values, personal habits, backgrounds and expectations."

• *Interpersonal issues.* Five other content areas concern the way partners interact with each other, or their interpersonal relationship: Communication, Conflict Resolution, the Sexual Relationship, the Role Relationship, and Children and Parenting. "Problematic areas in couple relationships often include: communication, sex, marital roles and conflict."

• *External issues.* Three content areas are identified as outside influences on couple functioning: Financial Management, Family/Friends, and Family of Origin.

Treatment and Referral Options

If the counselor has identified a couple as seriously conflicted or dysfunctional, he or she has at least three options. Of course, these options vary in specific instances depending on the background, clinical experience, and qualifications of the premarital counselor.

The first option is for the couple to complete the premarital counseling process as described in Chapters Three, Four, and Five of this book. During that process, the couple is treated as if they are not seriously conflicted or dysfunctional; the counseling process in most ways ignores or overlooks their dysfunction. We do not believe that this is an appropriate treatment for relationship dysfunction. However, when the couple is not aware of the dysfunction or conflict or the counselor is not alert to the signs of conflict and dysfunction, such blind counseling likely occurs.

A second option open to the counselor who is confronted with a conflictual or dysfunctional couple is to refer that couple to another counselor or therapist. A referral should be made whenever the counselor does not have the time or training to work with the couple appropriately. A referral to a professional who is better trained in dealing with interpersonal conflict and couple dysfunction is desirable. Even if the premarital and remarital counselor has the training, experience, and skills to treat the couple, since such couples represent a minority of the premarital and remarital counseling population, the counselor may choose to refer them because of a lack of time or interest in working with them.

The conscientious premarital and remarital counselor will establish a working relationship with professionals who can serve as referral sources. Although the availability of referral sources will vary in localities, counselors can find professionals who are competent in working with conflicted and dysfunctional premarital and remarital couples by contacting the American Association for Marriage and Family Therapy (AAMFT). The national office for the AAMFT provides a referral list of clinical members in specific geographical regions.[5]

A third option available to the premarital counselor confronted with a dysfunctional premarital couple is to treat the couple in counseling or therapy according to their specific dynamics. The dysfunction or serious problems may be identified during the counseling processes of the DRH and FOE (see Chapters Four and Five). In such cases, the counseling is extended and follows the therapeutic techniques used with marital conflict and dysfunction. It is beyond the scope of this book to detail specifically the treatment of the dysfunctional or seriously conflicted premarital or remarital couple.

In this chapter we have discussed counseling in special premarital and remarital situations including very young and older first marriages, forced marriages, and conflicted relationships. While these situations do not occur in most counseling cases, they will likely be encountered by the counselor.

In this book we have presented what we consider to be current knowledge and approaches to premarital and remarital counseling. We presented a detailed approach to the counseling process, and concluded with a discussion of specific topics and interventions. We hope that the reader has been stimulated to adopt and adapt some of the ideas discussed.

Notes

Chapter One

1. U.S. Bureau of the Census. (1995). *Statistical abstract of the United States, 1995* (115th ed.). Washington, DC.
2. Adams, T. R. (1996). *LDS counselor ratings of problems occurring among LDS premarital and remarital couples.* Unpublished master's thesis, Brigham Young University; Jones, E. F., & Stahmann, R. F. (1994). Clergy beliefs, preparation, and practice in premarital counseling. *The Journal of Pastoral Care, 48*(2), 181–186; and Summers, J. R., & Cunningham, J. L. (1989). Premarital counseling by clergy: A key link between church and family. *Family Science Review, 2*(4), 327–336.
3. *Marriage preparation in the Catholic church: Getting it right.* (1995). Creighton University, Center for Marriage and Family.
4. National Center for Health Statistics. (1996). *Births, marriages, divorces, and deaths for 1995, 44*(12). Hyattsville, MD: Public Health Service. Monthly vital statistics report.
5. Nichols, W. C. (1992). *The AAMFT: Fifty years of marital and family therapy.* Washington, D.C.: American Association for Marriage and Family Therapy.
6. Rutledge, A. L. (1966). *Premarital counseling.* Cambridge, MA: Schenkman.
7. Johnson, P. E. (1953). *Psychology of pastoral care.* Nashville, TN: Abingdon Press.
8. Butterfield, O. M. (1956). *Planning for marriage.* New York: Van Nostrand Reinhold.
9. Ellis, A. (1961). *Creative marriage.* New York: Institute for Rational Living.
10. Mace, D. R. (1972). *We can have better marriages if we really want them.* Nashville, TN: Abingdon Press.
11. Lewis, R. A., & Spanier, G. B. (1979). Theorizing about the quality and stability of marriage. In W. R. Burr, R. Hill, I. F. Nye, & I. L. Reiss (Eds.), *Contemporary theories about the family* (Vol. 1, pp. 259–267). Old Tappan, NJ: Macmillan.
12. Larson, J. H., & Holman, T. B. (1994). Premarital predictors of marital quality and stability. *Family Relations, 43,* 228–237.
13. Ibid., pp. 228–229.

Chapter Two

1. Whitaker, C. A., & Keith, D. V. (1977). Counseling the dissolving marriage. In R. F. Stahmann & W. J. Hiebert (Eds.), *Klemer's counseling in marital and sexual problems: A clinician's handbook* (2nd ed., pp. 65–78). Baltimore: Williams & Wilkins.

2. See Gottman, J. (1994). *Why marriages succeed or fail.* New York: Simon & Schuster; see also Wallerstein, J. S., & Blakeslee, S. (1995). *The good marriage: How and why love lasts.* Boston: Houghton Mifflin.
3. Bowman, H. A., & Spanier, G. B. (1978). *Modern marriage.* New York: McGraw-Hill.
4. Guldner, C. A. (1971). The post-marital: An alternative to premarital counseling. *Family Coordinator, 20,* 115–119.

Chapter Three
1. Stahmann, R. F., & Hiebert, W. J. (1987). *Premarital counseling: The professional's handbook.* San Francisco: New Lexington Press.
2. Stahmann, R. F., & Barclay-Cope, A. (1977). Premarital counseling: An overview. In R. F. Stahmann & W. J. Hiebert (Eds.), *Klemer's counseling in marital and sexual problems: A clinician's handbook* (2nd ed., pp. 295–303). Baltimore: Williams & Wilkins.

Chapter Four
1. Hiebert, W. J., Gillespie, J. P., & Stahmann, R. F. (1993). *Dynamic assessment in couple therapy.* San Francisco: New Lexington Press.

Chapter Five
1. Framo, J. L. (1996). A personal retrospective of the family therapy field: Then and now. *Journal of Marital and Family Therapy, 22,* 289–316.
2. McGoldrick, M., & Gerson, R. (1985). *Genograms in family assessment.* New York: Norton.
3. See books such as: Leman, K. (1991). *Were you born for each other?* New York: Delacorte Press; Hoopes, M. H., & Harper, J. M. (1989). *Birth order and sibling position in family therapy.* Gaithersburg, MD: Aspen; and Tolman, W. (1976). *Family constellation.* New York: Springer.

Chapter Six
1. Stahmann, R. F. (1996). Marriage Preparation Research Project. 240 TLRB, Brigham Young University, Provo, UT 84602.
2. Life Innovations, P.O. Box 190, Minneapolis, MN 55440–0190 (Tel. 800–331–1661; FAX 612–331–2318).
3. See Olson, D. H. (1996). *PREPARE/ENRICH counselor's manual.* Minneapolis, MN: Life Innovations. Inventory descriptions and information used with permission.
4. Ibid., p. 71.
5. FOCCUS is published by Family Life Office, 3214 N. 60th Street, Omaha, NE 68104 (Tel. 402–551–9003).
6. Markey, B., Micheletto, M., & Becker, A. (1985). *FOCCUS: Facilitator manual.* Omaha, NE: Archdiocese of Omaha, Family Life Office.
7. Williams, L., & Jurich, J. (1995). Predicting marital success after five years: Assessing the predictive validity of FOCCUS. *Journal of Marital and Family Therapy, 21,* 141–153.
8. Parish Data Systems, Inc., 14425 N. 19th Avenue, Phoenix, AZ 85023 (Tel. 800–999–7148).
9. Stahmann & Hiebert. (1987).

Chapter Seven

1. Whitaker, C. A. & Keith, D. V. (1984). Counseling the dissolving marriage. In R. F. Stahmann & W. J. Hiebert (Eds.), *Counseling in marital and sexual problems.* San Francisco: New Lexington Press.
2. Pasley, K., Dollahite, D. C., & Ihinger-Tallman, M. (1993). Clinical applications of research findings on the spouse and stepparent roles in remarriage. *Family Relations, 42,* 315–322.
3. Pasley, K., Rhoden, L., Visher, E. B., & Visher, J. S. (1996). Successful stepfamily therapy: Clients' perspectives. *Journal of Marital and Family Therapy, 22,* 343–357.
4. Ibid., p. 352.

Chapter Nine

1. Stahmann, R. F., & Rogers, N. A. (1994). *Clergy premarital counselors' ratings of problems occurring among first marriages and remarriages.* Paper presented at the annual meeting of the National Council on Family Relations, Minneapolis, MN.
2. Silliman, B., & Schumm, W. R. (1989). Topics of interest in premarital counseling: Clients' views. *Journal of Sex and Marital Therapy, 15,* 199–205.
3. Ibid., p. 204.
4. Pasley, Rhoden, Visher, & Visher. (1996).
5. Lederer, W. J. (1981). *Marital choices.* New York: Norton.
6. Simon, S. B. (1974). *Meeting yourself halfway.* Niles, IL: Argus.
7. Stuart, R. B. (1980). *Helping couples change: A social learning approach to marital therapy.* New York: Guilford Press.
8. Markman, H., Stanley, S., & Blumberg, S. L. (1994). *Fighting for your marriage: Positive steps for preventing divorce and preserving a lasting love.* San Francisco: Jossey-Bass. Videotapes are also available for counselor training or for premarital and remarital counseling or workshops (Tel. 800–366–0166).

Chapter Ten

1. Stahmann, R. F. (in press). Therapists must be EXPLISSIT. In T. S. Nelson & T. S. Trepper (Eds.), *101 interventions in family therapy* (Vol. 2). Binghamton, NY: Haworth Press.

Chapter Eleven

1. Albrecht, S. L., Bahr, H. M., & Goodman, K. L. (1983). *Divorce and remarriage: Problems, adaptations, and adjustments.* Westport, CT: Greenwood Press.
2. Ibid., p. 77.
3. Knox, D. (1979). *Exploring marriage and the family.* Glenview, IL: Scott, Foresman.
4. Olson. (1996). Pp. 12–14. Quotes used with permission.
5. AAMFT, 1133 15th Street NW, Suite 300, Washington, DC 20005–2710 (Tel. 202–452–0109).

About the Authors

Robert F. Stahmann, Ph.D., is professor of family sciences in the marriage and family therapy graduate programs at Brigham Young University in Provo, Utah. He is a fellow and approved supervisor in the American Association for Marriage and Family Therapy; a certified family life educator in the National Council on Family Relations; and a certified sex therapist in the American Association of Sex Educators, Counselors, and Therapists. In addition, he is a member of the American Association of Christian Counselors and the American Counseling Association. Dr. Stahmann has published numerous professional articles and reviews. He is coauthor with William J. Hiebert and Joseph P. Gillespie of *Dynamic Assessment in Couple Therapy* (1993), and is coauthor of four other books.

William J. Hiebert, S.T.M., is executive director of the Marriage and Family Counseling Service in Rock Island, Illinois. He also serves as adjunct professor of pastoral counseling at the University of Dubuque Theological Seminary in Dubuque, Iowa. He is a fellow and approved supervisor in the American Association for Marriage and Family Therapy, and a member of the American Family Therapy Academy. Professor Hiebert is coauthor with Robert F. Stahmann and Joseph P. Gillespie of *Dynamic Assessment in Couple Therapy* (1993) and has authored or coauthored five other books.

Index

Affection: and intimacy, 192; assessed in Dynamic Relationship History, 69, 75–76

Age at marriage: first marriages, 3; remarriages, 3; as special focus, 199–200

American Association of Marriage and Family Counselors, 11

American Association for Marriage and Family Therapy (AAMFT), referral source, 207

Arguments, frequency, 203

Assessment in premarital counseling. *See* Dynamic Relationship History; Instrumentation

Bibliotherapy, 53–54

Blumberg, S., 189

Bonding, 10, 32–34, 68; assessed in Dynamic Relationship History, 68, 77

Budget, 183–186; and PREPARE and PREPARE-MC, 183–184

Butterfield, O., 12

Catholic church: use of counseling team, 17; use of FOCCUS inventory, 130

Children, 122, 131–132, 150

Clergy: estimates of client problems by, 172–174; in group counseling, 142; as premarital and remarital counselor, 5, 7–9, 40–45; in wedding preparation, 106–108

Client satisfaction: premarital counseling, 4, 174; remarried stepparents, 175

Commitment, assessed in Dynamic Relationship History, 77–78; assessed in group counseling, 166

Communication: assessed in Dynamic Relationship History, 69, 71–72; and decision making, 186–189; "I" statements, 180; and white and red bean exercise, 177–180

Conflict: assessed in Dynamic Relation-

ship History, 69, 71–73, 205; assessed by inventories, 205

Conjoint premarital counseling, 48–49, 55–56; and serious conflict, 204–207

Counseling: expectations and EXPLISSIT model, 190–193; preventive orientation, 10; repair orientation, 10

Couple and Family Map, 99

Courtship, reasons to prolong, 201–202

Decision making, 79; communication exercise, 186–189

Decourting, 140

Dependency: assessed in Dynamic Relationship History, 78; and bonding, 32–33

Dimensions of marriage, 29–31

Divorce rate, 5, 199

Dollahite, D., 149

Dyadic questioning, 64–66

Dynamic Relationship History (DRH): definition, 56, 60, 83; rationale, 57–58, 60–63; and strengthening courtship, 202–203; technique, 63–83; uncovering conflict, 205

Ellis, A., 13

Expectations of counseling: clients, 44, 55–56; congregations, 40–44; counselor, 55–56; and EXPLISSIT model, 191–193; state, 42

Expectations about marriage: 22–24; for couple, 176–177; for husband, 176; for wife, 176

EXPLISSIT model: and levels of counseling, 190–191; and sexuality, 191–193

Facilitation Open Couple Communication, Understanding and Study (FOCCUS), 58, 70, 81; areas assessed by, 131–133; described, 130–131; goals of, 130; in